Happiness is Chosen Wisely

3300 Axioms of
Self-Evident Truths

BYER

The ideas and opinions expressed in this book are the author's own and are not meant to advise or instruct, but are for entertainment purposes only. Any resemblance to other books, articles, or online material by other authors is entirely coincidental.

Reproduction or utilization of this work in any form, by any means now known or hereinafter invented, including, but not limited to, xerography, photocopying and recording, podcasting, and in any known storage and retrieval system, is forbidden without permission from the copyright holder.

The text for this book was set in Garamond.

Printed and bound in the United States of America.

10 9 8 7 6 5 4 3 2

Happiness is Chosen Wisely/BYER/1st edition

Summary:
Choosing happiness over pleasure through wisdom and enlightenment.

[1. Self-help/Personal growth/happiness; 2.Reference/Quotations]

Cover design and copyright: SelfPubBookCovers.com/Viergacht

All rights reserved.

ISBN-13: 978-0692966563
ISBN-10: 0692966560

Copyright © 2017 BYER

Happiness
is
Chosen Wisely

3300 Axioms of
Self-Evident Truths

BYER

Table of Contents

1. Why this book: To understand life and myself 7
2. Cause and effect: We are the cause of the effects 11
3. Desire and fear: Fight fear and flee desire 17
4. Human nature: We are self-destructive 44
5. Pleasure: Our world seeks pleasure 58
6. Society: The effects of our dysfunction 77
7. Nature: All is by the laws of nature 95
8. Truth: Always fallen on deaf ears 100
9. Awareness: Life's accomplishment is awareness 113
10. Consciousness and conscience: Life's within our consciousness ... 125
11. Higher thinking: The degree of our happiness 133
12. Wisdom: To produce a given event 160
13. Peace: Just peace from ourselves 202
14. Harmony: Stop denying the truth 214
15. Simplicity: Our greatness is simplicity 221
16. Freedom: Controlled by our unknown 225
17. Alone: To become all-one 234
18. Happiness: Give up desire to have happiness 245
19. Enlightenment: Our wisdom back upon our minds function 284
20. Heaven: We are in heaven now 313
21. Profound conclusion:
    Pleasure is meaningless and happiness is meaningful 322

ACKNOWLEDGMENT

After many attempts and failures at acquiring a publisher to help self-publish this book, my deepest respect and gratitude goes to Sheffield Publications for their professionalism in allowing the writer's words to be told.

CHAPTER ONE

WHY THIS BOOK?
To understand life and myself

This book is the result of my writing for discovery, to better understand life and myself in order to become contented and happy.

While working in engineering for many years and advancing my career to become a manager of larger projects and sales, I started noticing my personal life was in complete disarray. This was from working longer hours out of town away from my family; I was drinking too much, using drugs, and some other indiscretions. That's when I thought, "Why don't I just turn my successful project managing skills back upon my own mind's functioning and start managing myself as a self-styled project?" This was a point in my life when my higher thinking caught up with my lower desire for pleasure and fear of pain. That's also when I quit my career and started the search for a deliberate life of contentment and happiness to where I am at today.

This book is meant to define the differences between pleasure and happiness as two distinct opposite states of mind. While pleasure is the effect of our desires as an instinctive motivational process, all emotions originate in our consciousness as a desire, which then results in stress, anxiety and despair (S.A.D.) in order to acquire the pleasure we desired in the first place, with an added fear of loss. For all pleasures last but a short time because of hedonic adaptation and are required to be reinforced at a later time over and over as a closed loop system. This requires us to give pleasure to others in order to receive pleasure in return, either by mutually pleasurable benefits of a social barter system or paying someone to give us what we desire. Happiness, on the other hand, is our mind's higher thinking that first must override our instinctive motivations for pleasure to be realized in our lives at all. The cause of happiness is peace, calm, tranquility, bliss and harmony but the effects are the same as the cause. This is our absence of desire from our higher thinking, wisdom, and enlightenment without any stress, anxiety or despair at all.

Our minds are like a coin. One side of the coin is tails. It's the emotional side that's always motivated toward what looks, tastes, feels, sounds, and smells pleasurable. While the other side of the coin is heads: that's our reason and logic for what's best for us to become happy and contented. Both these sides occupy the same brain, but are looking out at our lives in two opposite directions, often at the same times of our lives. Thus lays the struggle between our emotions and higher thinking.

Our desires are a fantasy from the body's ability to produce chemicals that feel good without any logical reason; generally all that feels good is not good for us. We tend to rely on emotion as opposed to reason, which is why we have suffering in our lives. The definition of enlightenment does not say what it is, but instead how to acquire enlightenment: Questioning of traditional doctrines and values, tendency toward individualism, emphasis on the idea of universal human progress, method of science, use of reason. That's what this book is meant to address, the result of our higher thinking is for the enjoyment of happiness all our lives without the burden of desires or fears.

This book is an abridged version of a much larger text, while still retaining the sense of the original. These 3300 axioms are short propositions of self-evident truths and common sense that can be read anytime out of context of the whole. They are all meant to be original writings and any resemblance to other books is unintentional.

"Life tests us all, but it is up to us to test ourselves. All self-evident truths and common sense are the two best friends we will ever have."

This book is the result of many years of a self-driven quest to read and write for discovery. The bulk of this writing was handwritten by lamplight early in the mornings on a boat. Far removed from the influences of a desire for pleasure or fear of pain that society, family, or friends afford, in solitude, but not lonely so as to see life and myself clearly. My first subject of study was the main religions of the world, but I could not find definitive reasons or logic for their beliefs. The second subject of study was philosophy and this was much more informative. Then at the period known as the "Age of Enlightenment," and specifically Brock Spinoza wrote: "Men think themselves free because they are conscious of their actions, but ignorant of the causes of these actions," also "They always act in accordance with the laws of their nature and for that reason think themselves free." This has prompted the third and last subject of study that this book is about, human behavior that was the cause of the first two subjects of religion and philosophy in the first place. We may have gotten more instructions on how a computer system functions than on how our brain system functions. Then since our mind is the cause of all of life's experiences as the effects, we rarely try to understand the reasons for our decisions. To become free we must control what controls us and that is us. The scientific study of neurology is the neuropathic system that is a higher advanced form of instinct establishing our value system, with over 50 complex chemical molecules of neurons. The best known are: Dopamine, Norepinephrine, Serotonin, Cortisol, Oxytocin, Vasopressin, which neuroscience researchers are unraveling for their combinations and related effects on our reward and punishment responses for feelings of wellbeing. The entire motivational system originates at the Protoself (Wikipedia) lower level of our brain stem, rather than at the cerebral cortex or higher thinking.

This is not thinking at all, just emotions that are the cause of our decisions for desire or fear. Then to be human, as opposed to any other species, was to acquire our higher thinking over our instinctual emotions that are diametrically opposed to each other, resulting in questionable life decisions.

The human species has the most complex mind on this earth yet we get virtually no instruction on how it works. The human race is noticeably dysfunctional in many ways, but the lack of knowledge or understanding of itself is not questioned. The educational system seems to be just teaching what it was taught itself. The greatest demand for improvement is for us as a society to make more money and not to become more knowledgeable of ourselves so we could make better life decisions. That would be meaningful and not meaningless. We may also get more instruction on how to drive a car than we do on how to drive our minds. A race car driver knows how their car was designed, operates, and its limitations so as to be a better race car driver. Wouldn't that same logic apply toward humans as well if we know how our minds worked? Wouldn't we be able to make our lives run better by planning and understanding our weaknesses and strengths, when all our instructions or plans for a decision is "if it feels, sounds, tastes, looks and smells good then we should do it?"

The biggest and best kept secret in our lives seems to be how our minds work because our mind has a reluctance to know itself. We are concentrating on the outside world and the effects of our desires, but never want to really learn what the cause of those effects were. We go to great extent to get an education so as to influence each other by those credentials, maybe for fame or fortune, but mostly to make greater income so as to have more pleasure and less fear of pain. The fictional books read out of school are for our personal enjoyment for pleasure or entertainment. Those that are nonfiction are of many other subjects, but few are self-discovery.

Our species is blind to itself yet we all operate our own minds without any instruction or knowledge, as a child does from birth till death: if it feels good we want to do it. We have learned very little about ourselves, which is why history always repeats itself. The cause of the problems of the entire human race is the cause of the motivations of our own life's race; that we are the cause of the effect of our lives from our emotional responses and not our higher thinking. Then our lives would become the effects of our higher thinking, instead of our lowest desires for pleasure or fear of pain, which is the result of ego, lust and fear. In order to counteract our instinctive emotions we must fight and flee, that's to fight fear and flee pleasure. This is to become free from ourselves now, not in maybe some afterlife in another world.

By utilizing our higher thinking we can make our lives a better place to be by controlling ourselves and not to be controlled by some unknown aspect of our outdated instinctual emotions, which are harmful in this advanced culture, but not advanced emotional state of mind. Our highest purpose is found through experience, awareness, and introspection, so as to direct ourselves to become the cause of our life's motivations for happiness. That is peace, calm, tranquility, bliss and harmony, which is heaven on earth. This can be accomplished through knowledge, influence and will: we can acquire the wisdom in order to be happy without pleasure or pain that leads to suffering. We may be unaware of the capacity of directing ourselves that's either better for happiness or worse for pleasure. Either from feelings of emotions or reasoning of our minds, life will unfold as effects now. The present moment as we determined it, is either meaningful or meaningless.

CHAPTER TWO

CAUSE AND EFFECT:
We are the cause of the effects

1.
The direction of life's course is to be determined by the soundness of our decisions, for we are the cause of the effects of our life.

2.
Today is the effects of yesterday and the cause of tomorrow.

3.
Our higher mental thoughts are of life's causes and not just life's effects.

4.
Our mind's ability to become the cause of our motivations, and not the effects of Nature's motivation that's already in us.

5.
The effects in life are simplistic and our main concern, but the cause will evade us for as long as we are not thinking.

6.
Until we know the cause of life's struggles, we will always endure pain and suffering.

7.
We are so consumed with life's out-sights, we have no time for life's insights.

8.
Instinctive motivations are the unknown causes of all the effects we experience of life.

9.
Life gets easier as we learn how the mind sees life, ourselves; for the cause of our futures are the effects of our minds now.

10.
When we have a problem, just consider we may be the cause.

11.
Let peace, calmness, tranquility, blissfulness and harmony produce the results of peace, calmness, tranquility, blissfulness and harmony, for one must precede the other as in cause and effect.

12.
We are the cause of our discomfort and source of our unhappiness.

13.
We don't have to die to go to heaven when we know we are there now. We may know this when we ask, "What comes first, the cause or the effect?"

14.
When we only feel the effects we will never think to see the cause.

15.
All of humanity's faults will live on because they produce life, but also sustain life as its cause and effect.

16.
True freedom of choice is the cause of its effects.

17.
We live in the effects of life instead of in the cause.

18.
Since our mind is the cause of all our life's experiences as the effects, why do we rarely try to understand the cause of our whole life's courses beginning?

19.
Lower instinctual motivations, or our higher thinking motivations, will be the cause of the effects of our lives.

20.
Are we the cause of the life we live?

21.
We can't stop life's effects on us until we become the cause of our own effects on us.

22.
The awareness of our upper level of mental life is the cause of reason for the cause of our life, and not the effects of nature's motivations within us.

23.
Those who are conscious of the causes of their lives can then live their own effects.

24.
When we know the cause of our discontented effects, we can then become the cause of our contented effects.

25.
We are the cause of our discontent, so must become the cause of our contentment.

26.
Our most important outlook on life turns out to begin from our in-look into our minds. To enlighten and guide our thinking, we become as in cause and effect.

27.
An uneasy life is hurried, busy, and full of annoyances, while an easy life is peaceful, calm and relaxed. One is the effects of desire and the other is the cause of happiness.

28.
To see life's effects is not the same as seeing life's causes.

29.
Peace, calm, and tranquility are the cause and bliss; harmony and heaven is the effect. This is our happiness from cause to effect.

30.
It is pathetic to only see the effects of life and not the cause.

31.
All pleasure has costs, either emotional or financial, while happiness cause is also its effects of peace, calm, tranquility and harmony. Bliss is heaven.

32.
Our future realities reside within us as motivational results.

33.
We tend to see life as outside of us and not the effects of our lack of thinking.

34.
Are we happy now with the effects of our lives? Because we are always the cause. Until we know this, we will always be the effects of life's causes.

35.
When our lives are peaceful and calm, we must be the cause over our life's effects.

36.
Without knowing we are the cause of life's problems, we're unable to become a solution.

37.
We will not change until we change. This is the hardest thing to see much less do. We may see the effects we want, but not the cause that's within us.

38.
We could become the cause of our own effects when we establish our own motivations instead of the body's instinctive motivations.

39.
When we see life clearly, life becomes clearer. This is cause and effect from our wisdom and not from unknown forces beyond our command and control.

40.
It is either heaven or hell on earth. This is our choice for aren't we the cause of all the effects in our life?

41.
To know through careful observation the cause and not its effects so we might become the cause to our own life's effect.

42.
We know our lives by unthinking and not by thinking. We are the cause of the effects of our life.

43.
When we know life then we know ourselves. When we know this, we become the cause of the effects of our lives, too.

44.
We are the effects of either knowing or feeling ourselves clearly. That's knowing with our mind's eye and not just feeling.

45.
We all know the effects of not thinking, but what is the cause of our thinking?

46.
Nature is the cause of our basic motivations and our lives are the effects. Our higher thinking could become the cause of our lives in the future.

47.
We are the effects of our current state of mind.

48.
When we think about life it gets easier.

49.
Our limitations are preserved when we seek the effects, but our limitations are removed when we seek the causes.

50.
We have to be peaceful to find peacefulness; we have to be calm to find calmness; we have to be tranquil to find tranquility. In this way we are the cause of the effects of our life.

51.
A balance between opposing forces is reason over emotion, which will result in quite, restful inaction.

52.
Self-control will result in a minimalist lifestyle, and less wanted is more leisure.

53.
Self-knowledge will result in self-mastery that is cause and effect.

54.
For every loss we have our gains. We must lose our innocence to have our wisdom, we must lose our desire to have our happiness; we must lose our life to have had life.

55.
Our thinking is stopped in midair when a desire flies by.

56.
Our desire says yes, our wisdom says no, our desire says yes yes yes, our wisdom is silenced.

57.
All of life's problems start with desire.

58.
We will do all things imaginable for all desires imaginable.

CHAPTER THREE

DESIRE AND FEAR:
Fight fear and flee desire

1.
We are slaves to our desires and hostage from our fears. Then we should fight fear and flee desire.

2.
We can never be wise if we are always controlled by our desires and fears.

3.
We must learn how to oppose our basic desires because to know the unknown is to just know ourselves.

4.
Let's not fool ourselves any more. We don't know what to do in life and never did. We just do what feels good.

5.
All desires are unhappiness with our lives now because of feeling and not thinking.

6.
The toll for desire or fear is the toil of our lives.

7.
I have desire and fear, but they don't have me.

8.
If desire and fear is all we look for, then that's all we'll find.

9.
Our higher thinking is in silent bondage to all of our desires and fears.

10.
When we are not happy, then we are suffering from desire or fear.

11.
We are trapped when we trade old pleasures for new because we cannot get away from ourselves.

12.
We cannot think clearly when all we want is to have fun. Only when we stop desiring or fearing can we ever think clearly.

13.
We don't know what our higher thinking is all about because all we know for sure is our desires and fears.

14.
All life struggles from the effects of our instinctive emotions that desire and fear causes.

15.
We are up, we are down, we are all around. Running here, running there. Yet, we can't seem to fathom the depth of our despair is desire.

16.
Any and all desires shouldn't override our higher thinking, but we are controlled by our limitations instead of our strengths.

17.
We will suffer as long as our motivation for desire and fear controls our thinking.

18.
The gates to all bondage are desire and fear.

19.
When we can let go of our desires and fears, we'll have found what's really important was life.

20.
Our greatest accomplishment is to acquire peace from our desires and fears.

21.
We want to appease our desires in order to feel satisfied, but when we limit our desires, there is nothing that has to be done.

22.
We desire what is meaningless and we reject what is meaningful. We must let go of our desires and fears to embrace our freedom and happiness.

23.
If we never seem to get enough of what we desire, why will that make us happy?

24.
We are well aware of what we know, but unaware of what we don't know because we have no desire to find out.

25.
We are seeking our desires, but not the reason for our desires in order to understand life's causes.

26.
When we do what we desire that will leave us ignorant of the rest.

27.
We must pay for our desires, but we already own our fears.

28.
Our desire for pleasure or fear of pain is no better than all life on earth when we have so much more potential just wasted.

29.
When our minds are unknown to us, then so is the cause of our desires and fears.

30.
Thoughts derived from desire or fear can't be substantiated by reason or logic. We are left defenseless to a life of emotions and blown about by those winds.

31.
The homeless state is traveling freely from place to place. This is the effects of no desires or fear.

32.
When we limit our desires, we will gain happiness to that same degree.

33.
Desire or fear will hasten our demise. The enemy among us all is not some outside threat but lies within us.

34.
All life's struggles seem to be over desire without us even knowing.

35.
Desire and fear rule all of life, but through reason and logic we may rule ourselves.

36.
Desire without thinking is self-destructive to our bodies and minds.

37.
Desire and fear is all consuming as a hindrance to our peace of mind.

38.
By always longing for what is missing, we are unaware of what we have. All desire is demanding.

39.
We will feel all desires and fears from birth till death without ever knowing ourselves.

40.
Firmness of mind is will over ourselves; for all courage may be lost in the presence of desire or fear.

41.
We feel it's too much trouble to think when it's much easier to just feel good. That's all we desire anyway. This is the barrier to enter into a new way of thinking.

42.
We could do anything we want, but we chose to become a prisoner of our desires and fears all the days of our lives.

43.
We are looking for what we want, but not realizing that's self-limiting. This is because our basic motivation is not thinking, but desire.

44.
Our emotions are like a pack of wild animals, out of control by demanding to be fulfilled now.

45.
Desire is both puzzling and mystifying, because it doesn't require any thought. The purpose is concealing its true meaning. This is done unconsciously at our expense.

46.
Ours is not a lifestyle of choice. We all choose from desires, not for reasons. This is done unconsciously as we will our life forward.

47.
To let go of all that we desire or fear is the path least traveled.

48.
We look past all the present truths to only see distant desires and fears in our future, and we get what we seek.

49.
When we do not desire or fear, nothing bothers us.

50.
Our height of desires will always precede our depths of despair.

51.
When we reason with our emotions, all our defenses are powerless to suffering.

52.
The punishment of desires is the payment it demands from us all our lives.

53.
We are up, we are down, but still we come back for another round. All desires are endless.

54.
When we know what we desire, we will know what's meaningless.

55.
We are so full of desires we can't see life clearly. This is what drives us to want more.

56.
We are servants of our desires or masters of ourselves.

57.
We can't see life's truths, but only what we desire instead.

58.
We have chosen the life we live and may not be happy because desire was a poor choice.

59.
While submitting to desire, we are forcing ourselves to a life of stress, anxiety, turmoil and despair so as to become disabled and handicapped.

60.
From desire we linger and then it is too late.

61.
Our life could become an act of free choice, but without compulsive desire or fear.

62.
We can't have pleasure for very long and it passes, but the desire is with us all our lives.

63.
Our lives go up, up into the air when we always desire and despair.

64.
Desire isn't our friend but our enemy, because without knowing this, we're our own prisoner until the end.

65.
Only when the barrier of desires and fears are realized can we think clearly.

66.
All our struggles in life are found to be within us from desire and fear.

67.
We are proof that desire and fear is not thinking, for whom among us is peaceful and calm.

68.
Everyone knows what desire is from birth till death, yet we never become satisfied with life that's in between.

69.
All desires pass so quickly it makes apprehension very difficult.

70.
We will all have to control our desires and fears in order to become the true masters of our lives now.

71.
When we are always controlled by desire or fear, but not our higher thinking, we're just doing what comes naturally.

72.
Who is our boss will become self-evident. That is desire and fear or peace and quiet?

73.
Our desires will cost us time, money and effort, but happiness doesn't.

74.
That desire, fear, takes all of our time and energy, and goes unnoticed to a closed mind. We must let light into the darkness of our minds.

75.
We must deal with the absence of desire in order to know happiness or contentment.

76.
Without our desires or fears, we are freed from our limitations to indulge our higher thinking.

77.
We cannot run away or even hide simply because of our desires and fears. Fleeing is the best solution to fighting life's struggles all life's long way.

78.
The homeless life is the life to be away from desires or fear, is also freedom from us.

79.
This is our last chance. If it feels good do not do it.

80.
We work to live or we live to work is self-imposed slavery, and without thinking, our masters were our desires and fears.

81.
All life instinctively motivates for desire and fear without knowing it, except humans have other abilities without knowing it either.

82.
We feel we are free for we know what we desire, but it's all basic instinctual motivations that are coursing through our minds and bodies.

83.
Desires far and away exceed our fears.

84.
We are happier when we are alone, at peace with ourselves, but we have more pleasure with others and our possessions. A slave to our desires doesn't know freedom.

85.
When we stop pursuing desires, we will be happy because happiness is the absence of desire.

86.
Desire be gone and leave me alone with my happiness.

87.
We feel we have our lives all figured out just because we know what we desire. That is really lower instinctive motivation and not our higher thinking.

88.
Desire isn't real. It's just a molecule of dopamine: a vision of delight, a fantasy of feeling.

89.
We desire what feels good more than the truth.

90.
Now desire and fear is not our friend, but in fact our enemy. We don't know this is why we can't be happy now.

91.
The problem with desire is it compels us not to think.

92.
We are possessed by desire and we are freed by happiness.

93.
All desire is unhappiness with life and with ourselves.

94.
Desire is a burden all our lives, but we are unaware.

95.
Beware of desire. It's a false positive.

96.
We don't seem to tire of being a slave to our desires.

97.
All our desires and fears will bar us from any higher thinking.

98.
We jump up and jump down and run all around when desire is all we know.

99.
When our mind can control motivations, we are free from desire and fear.

100.
We don't listen to what we don't desire to hear.

101.
Desire is a barrier to be peaceful, calm and tranquil.

102.
All our futures are to be determined by those thoughts today. Let those thoughts be deliberate and not just desire-driven.

103.
Beware of our attention toward a person or thing because it's an object of desire.

104.
Our higher thinking can become our motivational force instead of just desires or fears.

105.
We are slaves to our unbidden feelings of desire and fear yet still feel we are free to choose.

106.
We need not fear what threatens us as much as the threat we are to ourselves.

107.
What we desire and fear is harmful to us and the world because it's fun and exciting to our senses when we are feeling our way through life.

108.
We rationalize our desires by providing plausible but untrue reasons for our conduct.

109.
Victor of our thinking or victim of our desires?

110.
Desire is like a hammer because it beats us into submission.

111.
We are not free from our desires for pleasure otherwise we would be happy now.

112.
Desire is an irresistible impulse to perform an irrational act over and over again, while always expecting a different outcome of contentment and happiness.

113.
All desire stands in the way of enlightenment.

114.
When we desire to be the victor over others we will become the victim of ourselves.

115.
Desire is not worth the pain or suffering.

116.
Without a doubt, we would be self-limiting our ability to apply checks and balances to desires and fears.

117.
The desire for pleasure or fear of pain is meaningless because it's not thinking, it's feeling.

118.
An unhappy person always wants more, but a happy person doesn't want any more. If desire is discontentment, why would anyone want desire?

119.
Happiness is meaningful thinking while desire is meaningless feelings.

120.
We are the only ones who can reduce our desires because we would resent anyone from doing so.

121.
Desire is also our pain because all begins and ends with stress and anxiety; for all desires acquired leads to fears of loss.

122.
Our minds have a barrier to entry and it's called desire.

123.
When we think about them, our desire and fear are unbidden emotions.

124.
The human race has accomplished much, except authority over our desires or fears.

125.
We live the dream of our higher thinking or live the fantasy of our desire and fears.

126.
The burden of desire is also the burden of proof.

127.
We should fear ourselves above anything else for we will give much harm to our own being.

128.
Our desires simply trade one pleasure for another until the end of our days.

129.
The path to happiness is always calm and peaceful, but the freeway to desire is always stressful and anxious.

130.
When we do not want to know anything that we did not desire to know, we will have already eliminated what is meaningful.

131.
Freedom from desire is a way of life least traveled, but also the path of least resistance.

132.
Our freedom is a mutual concord to end hostilities within us. We won't become calm and internally undisturbed by emotions of desire and fear.

133.
We seem to be living out a human tragedy of our society's history without ever realizing our desires and fears were always the cause.

134.
All attachment to desire or fear is suffering.

135.
Our mind can control our emotions for happiness and not just desires all our lives.

136.
We are the effects of our desires and fears, not our thinking.

137.
We are slaves to our desires and prisoners of our fears. Without knowing this, we cannot gain our freedom from ourselves or others.

138.
Intelligence also limits our freedom because of our motivations.

139.
That absolute truth coupled with reason and logic should be the cause of our lives and not just our desires and fears.

140.
What we desire the most will likely be the cause of our death. We simply have less fear when it comes to desire.

141.
All that we desire is harmful to us yet we don't fear our desires. This shows we are not thinking.

142.
We give in to desires all our lives without thinking what's best for us.

143.
Our will exists for desire's sake and not our own.

144.
We will only dumb ourselves down by desire.

145.
Life is based on wealth or honor of each moment that's governed by desires and fears to our dishonor.

146.
Self-sufficiency is without desire or fear.

147.
Marriage is a function of becoming slaves to our desire for pleasure and fear of pain.

148.
What is good and what is good for us is the difference between desire and thinking.

149.
Our desire is the refusal to admit that death is true.

150.
Our imagination exists independently of the truth as a restriction on what is practical and common sense.

151.
Life will become meaningful when we're not motivated by desire or fear.

152.
When we are not controlled by desires or fears, we become free from ourselves.

153.
We must serve our desires for pleasure, but they do not serve us very well.

154.
More of what we do not need is desire.

155.
Desire is opposed to our best interests, without us thinking about truth our life is a fantasy.

156.
We are strangers within ourselves because we don't know or understand that our motivations are also harmful to our health.

157.
We simply do not know but we feel we must do.

158.
We are fooled by ourselves without knowing that we are trained by our desires.

159.
All desires are life's candy, for pleasures cannot be far behind.

160.
Happiness is peaceful and calm from the storms of our desires and fears.

161.
We are, in fact, not free when we do what we desire, because feels good is to be controlled by desire.

162.
There is a big difference in what feels good and what is good, for our best or worst is as close as our next decision.

163.
The abstinence of desire and fear is the only happiness we'll ever know.

164.
We must not leave this place if this place is making us happy. When it's not we are controlled by desires and fears.

165.
When we are always full of desire, we are empty inside.

166.
We do not know that desire is not thinking.

167.
We are so wrong all the time. We would be better off if we did the opposite of what we feel we should do.

168.
Desire is an irresistible impulse to perform an irrational act, which leads to even more. This in turn aggravates the first.

169.
Desire and fear are confining to an open mind.

170.
Desires are enticing and harmfully awaiting a chance to entrap.

171.
When we see life clearly, there will be no stress or anxiety or desire or fear.

172.
Life is a compromise when we don't know what we are doing and surrender to our desires or fears.

173.
What course do we have if our desires are a trap?

174.
We are blinded by desire so as not to see life clearly.

175.
Most success may come from failures. This is how we learn, but that doesn't apply to desire.

176.
Instincts are behind the obvious so it's hard to detect because all desire is in opposition to the spread of knowledge by a deliberate vagueness.

177.
We make the life for us we want, but very few make the life we need when we are captured by our desires.

178.
For the love of desire is our need for money. There is no compromise we can make that's too great.

179.
Our desires and fears are compulsive baggage.

180.
Without desire or fear, we can think clearly.

181.
Stress from desire is an inner impediment to free activity, expression, or function. This prohibits us from thinking of meaningful but just meaningless.

182.
We could make our decisions the best they could be by not restricting our thinking and going on doing our desires.

183.
We lack the desire to try to comprehend the scope of life's experience.

184.
Desire is a false positive as a fantasy from a neuropathic value system and not thinking.

185.
A more probable course in life may become evident even when the most pleasurable course is desirable.

186.
We must fight fear and flee desire in order to live a deliberate life.

187.
We desire what we cannot get away from. This is how we are captured.

188.
Our desire to possess a person or objects when realized is the loss of ourselves.

189.
We are so full of desire we have no time to think.

190.
We will become what we desired, or freed by much less.

191.
What could we have done without desire or fear?

192.
We desire to become fulfilled, but pleasure is only temporary and we must desire again, and again.

193.
Desire is appealing forcibly to our mind without reason.

194.
Desire or fear negates our clear thinking.

195.
A life of desire is a life of stress and anxiety.

196.
When we fear the unknown we will never know the unknown.

197.
What we desire to learn may also become self-limiting.

198.
All happiness is the elephant in the room that we cannot see because of our desires.

199.
Prudence is detecting that desires are a fantasy for escaping from ourselves.

200.
All desires are not necessary to become in control of our lives.

201.
Desire is not our friend.

202.
We are killing ourselves with love of everything we don't need but want.

203.
To be governed by desire makes no sense.

204.
Crazy is with desire or fear.

205.
We fear for fear's sake. This comes from us knowing we have not been harmed to the degrees we have expected.

206.
Fear is just another learning opportunity unless we're dead. Then we wouldn't have to ever be in the prison we have made for ourselves.

207.
The urgency of desire limits our ability to think about happiness.

208.
Desire and fear are our successes, but also the failures of mankind.

209.
We are defined by our weaknesses more than by our strengths because desire is not thinking.

210.
Desire only trumps happiness in our unconsciousness.

211.
Our physical appetites are an emotional desire for what others have.

212.
We have to see the futility of desire to find a more meaningful life.

213.
Mistakes are the progression of our desires and fears.

214.
Desire is a sensual, frivolous, amusement of delight.

215.
Desire or fear makes us unstable.

216.
We have a desire for pleasure but reason is not desirable; they're opposites so opposed to each other.

217.
Thinking is our highest ability but desire and fears are the natural instinctive motivations.

218.
The inability to control our emotions will result in arousal or agitation.

219.
We are drawn to the package instead of its contents for there is a credibility gap between our desires and their rewards.

220.
Our fears have conquered us without us thinking.

221.
We must let go of our desires to find ourselves, for we are the life we have created; but what of the life we've missed?

222.
We don't have authority over ourselves just because we know what we desire.

223.
We are fooled by our desire but not our thinking.

224.
Our mind will free us from suffering a life of desires, fears.

225.
We can all easily see what is missing in our lives, but we can't even see what isn't because we desire what we don't have, but don't know what we do have.

226.
We would see life much clearer from our higher thinking than our lower desires and fears.

227.
We are as bees to pollen; we fly from one desire to another.

228.
Life is a fantasy of our desire and fear.

229.
Our desire is opposed to common sense or truth and affects our whole self negatively.

230.
We err for desire and fear without thinking.

231.
We have thinking but it's motivated by desires without thinking.

232.
Desire or fear is limiting us from ever knowing a higher form of life.

233.
Fools have more desire than fear or will.

234.
A desirable life is a curse without thinking.

235.
We must learn to forego fleeting desires to attain happiness by a dominance of creative influence, rather than an instinctive response to our life.

236.
Our desires determined the life we have now and not our thinking.

237.
Suffering could lead to creativity or just more desire.

238.
We are free to have desire or fear, but not free to think what motivations are best.

239.
We are just an appendage of our instincts without knowing ourselves.

240.
Aren't our desires the cause of all the problems in our lives?

241.
Desire and fear are the alpha and omega of all life.

242.
The need for money is our physical and mental comfort, but the want for money is never ending desires and fears.

243.
What we want to know is what we desired to know and that is the problem.

244.
When we are only looking for what feels good isn't that not thinking at all? Our ability to think is always limited by our desires or fears.

245.
We simply do not think clearly when we're motivated by emotions.

246.
Peace is lonely, calm is boring, tranquil is agitating, bliss is nothingness. This is what desire is feeling about happiness.

247.
Desire is bored with enlightenment and enlightenment is bored with desire.

248.
Desire feels the life we have is the life we wanted. Wisdom knows the life we have is the life we needed.

249.
Happiness is increased at the degree that desire is decreased.

250.
Our time and money is not meaningful when spent on desire or fear.

251.
When all we seek is desire or fear that's all we will ever know.

252.
We may not feel that desires are meaningless because we are not thinking.

253.
We need to fear ourselves in order to be safe.

254.
We live in fear, or we could live in happiness.

255.
When we know our enemy lies within us is when our courage will begin.

256.
We are controlled by desire without reason or logic.

257.
Desire will hold us from becoming who we can become.

258.
Desire will always cause us problems, but we feel we must desire.

259.
Desire is meaningless because it's emotional and not thinking.

260.
All of life's dark matter is desire and fear.

261.
Without doubt we will be defenseless to our desires.

262.
Free time is an old friend for happiness; free time is an old enemy for desire.

263.
The obvious seems to escape our attention, that desires are opposed to our life, liberty and pursuit of happiness.

264.
All desires we must do, but thinking seems to be an option.

265.
We must watch out because all life's follies lie within our desires.

266.
When all self-interests are for desires, there is no freedom of thoughts, thus actions.

267.
There is a wall to happiness and it's called desire.

268.
With all the desires we've ever wanted, we are still not happy.

269.
We desire to know of all things, but to know ourselves is undesirable.

270.
We are killing ourselves with desire.

271.
Our insight into human nature is an awareness of our potential dangers.

272.
Just to overcome our desires is the best skill of all.

273.
What we desire all our lives is what's most harmful all our lives.

274.
All happiness is found just out of reach of desires.

275.
We accept all that is desirable and reject all that is not, without thinking.

276.
Desire is what defeats the strong and the weak in equal proportions.

277.
We become satisfied when we're contented, but we are unsatisfied when we are discontented, for all contentment is without desire, status or possessions.

278.

All life is given in abundance; we take what we desired or feared but in doing so maybe we left the best behind.

279.

Desire takes from those who have so little and desire gives to those who have so much. All is done without question.

280.

We are clustered on the main roads of life then desire and fear is all we wanted to know.

281.

There is always discontent in desire for what others possess, but if we think we have enough then we do have enough.

282.

Realism is hidden beyond the surface of what was seen as desire.

283.

We may desire to know of all things but when we think of what's most important, it's our lives and not things.

284.

Ask yourself what causes unhappiness and not what happiness is? And then you'll know that happiness is not desire.

285.

Life's struggle is from desire that overcomes the mind or the mind that overcomes desires.

286.

Desire is fun and exciting, but happiness is peaceful and calm, so which one would you choose?

287.

We forget desire's effects are stress, anxiety, turmoil and despair.

288.

All that we desired was harmful, when we think about it.

289.
We don't want to know what isn't desirable.

290.
All the desires we must seek will not be enough.

291.
When we rely on our emotions for all of life's decisions there will be desires then problems, pleasures and losses.

292.
We must desire stress because we want it all the time.

293.
Desires are fool's gold while happiness is golden.

CHAPTER FOUR

HUMAN NATURE:
We are self-destructive

1.
We are self-destructive through our human nature of attributes and qualities. Without knowing who we could become, we are who we are now.

2.
We can't get enough of what we don't need is our compulsive desire for pleasure.

3.
We feel our suffering may have been caused by others, but all that time we are the true cause of all our suffering. Until we see this, we can never change.

4.
Dysfunctional is humanity's way of life because we mate for looks and not for brains.

5.
Ignorance is maintained by ignoring all of life's lessons. This is the most prevailing human condition.

6.
We are least aware of all the forces that will determine our course in life.

7.
We don't even have to know very much to be judgmental, in fact it even helps.

8.
We don't know ourselves because that's not fun or exciting.

9.
We are where we planned, but we're not content where we are now.

10.
We must be functioning without actually thinking. How else can we explain why we do what we do?

11.
Our instinctual motives always control our higher thinking without us ever knowing, that's the problem.

12.
We can't think past ourselves for we are interfering with our progress by intentionally placing obstacles in our path.

13.
We are the effects of being human, but to become a thinking human would be unique.

14.
We confuse ourselves is why we're confused.

15.
We are driven by the unknown without thinking.

16.
Let's start from the beginning. That is us. We may never have gotten past that to find anything else.

17.
We don't know we are the problem or that we have one.

18.
We are conquered by what we conceived as a good idea.

19.
We seem to go through our lives without knowing why we do what we do.

20.
Most are interested in the effects of life, but not in the causes.

21.
We listen to what we want to hear and ignore the rest. Thus, the life we lead has been self-restricting and isolating.

22.
Let us begin from the beginning. Our most basic motivation is what compels us to do all that we do without knowing ourselves.

23.
Our choice is to feel good, but not to be good.

24.
Our human struggle is within us, but goes unnoticed.

25.
We are the monkey on our back except we haven't thought about that.

26.
If anything feels good, we want to do it and we don't think that may be a problem.

27.
We are naturally obsessed with the missing voids in our feeling good.

28.
We could become better if we weren't so normal.

29.
We will experience the effect of our actions without ever considering the causes of those goals. This is our essence and goes completely unrealized.

30.
That a single body part of another person can compel our entire life isn't thinking.

31.
We may think we are powerful, but are actually powerless over ourselves.

32.
We seem to get what we want in our lives, but we don't seem to want what we get. This is the human condition. Life's not as we wanted it to be.

33.
Ego, lust and fear is the essence of humanity. If they are your master, you will never know freedom or happiness.

34.
We do what we feel, but not what we think.

35.
We have a mind we don't have authority over, most of our lives.

36.
All of life's faults live within us.

37.
Life could be so simple, but we make it so complicated by overriding our thinking.

38.
Unreasonable is our irrational, illogical, normal selves.

39.
We've made all the choices in our life, and we are the results of them now.

40.
Let's be clear. We don't know what we're doing.

41.

Instinctive is unthinking; a bad guide through all life's choices because they don't involve reason and are just to remove tensions of the images we feel.

42.

We can see the world outside of ourselves easier than we can see within. This is why we know what we want, but we don't know why we do what we must do.

43.

We are all living the human condition, which is why we can't see ourselves clearly. We must go beyond ourselves in order to see us as we actually are.

44.

When we see a half moon, it's really a whole moon, but we can only see the light side. There is another side of life that's the light side, but we are living in the dark.

45.

Humanity has lost its way in life now because we don't know where we are now.

46.

That we are governed by unknown forces within us should give us concern, but doesn't. Then how can we ever expect a life that's any better?

47.

Some may find themselves, but most never even look.

48.

We are the joker in the wild cards that is life.

49.

We will have to be our own salvation because everyone else is just thinking of themselves.

50.
We must not worry about anything we can't change or we will become a victim of being human. We have no time to think because we are too busy reacting.

51.
We don't want to avoid life to its fullest. Like everyone else we just want to avoid being a fool over and over. Expecting different results but doing the same thing.

52.
We take ourselves for granted and will know sadness; that power is over the influence of ourselves.

53.
We are so busy wanting everything we see. We don't have time to think clearly and see the big picture.

54.
We live our lives in a mental default.

55.
We will become what we seek, simply an appendage of our ego, lust and fear.

56.
Unknown limitations rule our lives with an iron hand as our will.

57.
Our ability to see ourselves with a clear understanding of life is obscured by the overpowering intensity of our experiencing life itself.

58.
Life is more evident by looking at everyone else because we're destined not to see ourselves clearly.

59.
Our mind's a trap we are caught in when unaware.

60.
We are our own limitations without knowing it.

61.
We are sad when we don't know what we have, but just what we see we don't have.

62.
We are controlled by the darkness of our mind.

63.
We are all just functioning at our limitations.

64.
Our conditions of being deeply involved with emotions are very complicated and confusing.

65.
Denial is not our friend because life's truths will set us free.

66.
We seem to get what we want, but we don't need what we get.

67.
We know what we want, but if we don't think we'll never know any better.

68.
Life is good but we make it bad.

69.
We can't let go because our motivations are driving us without our knowledge of ourselves.

70.
Aren't our greatest temptations our greatest weaknesses?

71.
Our instinctive motivations are not reasonable life decisions.

72.
Our mind's a fantasy we are pre-disposed to serve.

73.
We are condemned by our compulsive needs.

74.
We are weak when we don't know it.

75.
Those who have the most to say are the least apt to listen.

76.
We take everything for granted, especially ungratefulness for being alive. We will always want more without ever knowing why.

77.
Those who talk the most seem to say the least. If essence is eternal, then silence is too.

78.
We don't know what we need; we just know what we want.

79.
When we express our feelings, it's most likely not meaningful.

80.
We don't have to judge another for they have already judged themselves and must live with themselves.

81.
Let go, I beg of myself. But myself controls me without letting go.

82.
To do wrong is ignorant and should be pitied not hated, but a fool knows right from wrong.

83.
The mind is clear, but the emotions are not. We can see this easier when we look at others we know.

84.
We are controlled by our weaknesses and not our strengths.

85.
We may see what's wrong with others, but we can't see what's wrong with us.

86.
Our lives are spent in quiet frustration. That's the result of compromise and regret.

87.
We may not know the difference between what feels good and is good.

88.
We may give in before we even know what's best for us because we're our worst enemy.

89.
Any and all forward progress is intentionally hampered by us placing obstacles in our own way.

90.
It is easier to find fault in others than it is to find fault in ourselves.

91.
Why we do what we do is because we can.

92.
For our own safety, we must change our own human nature.

93.
Our emotions are against the fiber of our being. That's detrimental to our health.

94.
When we don't give others pleasure, we are unwanted.

95.
Emotions are instinctual, thus not a free choice.

96.
We can run, but we can't hide from our weaknesses.

97.
We are receptive to our weaknesses, but not receptive to our strengths.

98.
The life we choose isn't free from the demands of our predisposition that controls everybody else.

99.
We talk so much, but we're not thinking.

100.
To fear you will be feared; to hate you will be hated; to love you will be loved.

101.
Our life's goal is to maximize our obsession by minimizing our thinking.

102.
We are compelled to do harm to ourselves because of the pleasures we desire.

103.
The more we rush the less we think.

104.
We will be governed by ignorance until we can talk about politics and religion logically without emotional biases.

105.
Desire and fear are opposed to wisdom: Therein lies the struggle of the human race.

106.
The more we are stimulated the more we want to be stimulated.

107.
We are victimizing ourselves without realizing it.

108.
We are dysfunctional because of our nature.

109.
When we can't consider we are the problem we may not find a solution.

110.
We are self-limiting because it feels good.

111.
Natural motivations rule all life without our knowledge.

112.
If you had more possessions you would be even less happy.

113.
We are harmed by our ego, lust, and fear.

114.
We do all things harmful without thinking.

115.
Our value system is based on unreasoned motivations.

116.
We have little desire to think, thus is humanity's dilemma.

117.
We are compelled to feel good, but to think is a choice.

118.
Life's struggle lies between our two minds: desire or happiness.

119.
Unbidden motivations will compel us through an unbidden life.

120.
Our motivations and actions are like reading a book of what not to do in order to become happy.

121.
People are running around without a clear understanding of themselves or life.

122.
Nature's laws rule all life, which is why so few are happy.

123.
We are compelled through life by unknown forces that will result in unhappiness.

124.
Emotional entanglements will result in irrational decisions.

125.
Slave of our fate goes unrealized because of emotions, but master of our fate goes realized because of thinking.

126.
We would be much better off by judging ourselves instead of others.

127.
We will not know what we don't want to know and that will be self-limiting.

128.
We hide from ourselves or we look for ourselves.

129.
We feel about life, but we don't think about life.

130.
The natural order of life is desire and fear for life's survival, that's an opposing force to all happiness.

131.
We will resent any others who have what we don't possess, either pleasure or happiness.

132.
If happiness does come from within why is everyone always looking outside for fun and excitement?

133.
When a strong person seeks another strong person to beat into submission this will only end badly for both.

134.
We seem to want to look better on the outside than we do on the inside.

135.
Those who know themselves are very few, but those who abuse themselves are many.

136.
We can find battles wherever we look for them or we can find friendships wherever we look for them.

137.
We will win hearts and minds with harmony or we will win fame or fortune with ambitions.

138.
There are few who want to know what not to do among so many who want to know what to do.

139.
We can see the faults in others easier than we can see the faults in ourselves.

140.
When we are full of success and boastful, we are full of ourselves.

141.
The angry person was defeated before they even got started because anger begets anger all their lives.

142.
Why is it we all know our weaknesses as though they were a friend and not the enemy that they are.

143.
We seem to be the most sure of ourselves when we know ourselves the least.

144.
To push back the darkness of our minds we will find more of the same, until the end of time.

145.
Our desires will neutralize our thinking in anticipation of pleasures return.

146.
We are proactive for pleasure and inactive for happiness.

147.
We spent every moment of every day in a desperate pursuit of pleasure.

148.
What would our lives be if we knew that pleasure is harmful to our health, wealth and happiness?

CHAPTER FIVE

PLEASURE:
Our world seeks pleasure

1.
We all come into this world seeking pleasure, and we go out of this world seeking pleasure. Unless we have figured that out, we haven't learned anything significant.

2.
The difference between pleasure and happiness is like the difference between prison and freedom.

3.
I have pleasure, but pleasure does not have me to the exclusion of reason and logic.

4.
The greatest pleasures gained are also the greatest freedoms lost.

5.
Wisdom goes to the grave while pleasure is for the moment.

6.
The greater pleasures we give up are our greatest victory over ourselves.

7.
Pleasure is a short term solution for a long term problem.

8.
Enlightenment is pleasure's enemy.

9.

The more pleasures we receive from others, the more we want from them, and the highest pleasures of all we call love.

10.

All that we add to our lives for pleasure, also subtracts from our happiness. When we decrease pleasure, we will increase happiness.

11.

Our life is an opportunity for pleasure or happiness, but we are controlled by one or freed by the other.

12.

Thinking is rarified air, rarely used in confirming any reason in pursuit of pleasures.

13.

We seem not to associate our discomfort to our desires for pleasure.

14.

Was pleasure worth our lives because that is what we spent?

15.

Letting go is smarter than holding on because we are fighting for pleasure when flight from pleasure is wiser.

16.

When we have pleasure, it draws us down to ourselves. But when we have happiness we are free from ourselves.

17.

Those that live for pleasure strive for something greater than themselves. Others strive for the greatness within themselves by thinking.

18.

One who favors restricting their power over others for pleasure will minimize their achievements to themselves.

19.

How can pleasure be meaningful when it's not from our higher thinking, but instinctual desires?

20.
All of our decisions should be determined by what's best for us as a whole and not for the pleasures of a single sub-component of our selves.

21.
Whenever we feel pleasure, it will become happiness; it's like chasing a rainbow.

22.
We are simply predestined from birth until death when we do what pleases us.

23.
All pleasure was the result of our refusal to accept the existence of truth or validity.

24.
When we aren't the driver, we become the driven. This is most difficult to see clearly because we don't look. The road least traveled is much less pleasurable.

25.
The cause of our bondage is ignorance and its effect is a desire for pleasure and a fear of pain.

26.
We have a natural aversion to anybody or anything that would diminish our pleasures.

27.
We may have never considered, do we possess our pleasures, our fears? Or, do they possess us without us knowing? While only one can be the master, the other is a slave.

28.
The course of all life is predisposed by pleasure and pain, without reason or logic.

29.

We must give pleasure to others in order to receive pleasure in return, but happiness we give to ourselves.

30.

We can have pleasure, but we can't let pleasure have us. This is only clear when we have the choice.

31.

Pleasure comes from not thinking because if we were thinking, we would know this. A child's mind only knows pain or pleasure; ours is still the same today.

32.

We are imprisoned by pleasures, but are freed by happiness.

33.

We will gladly trade our lives for the pleasures we desire without knowing the cause or a solution to our life's suffering.

34.

Pleasure determines our lives not thinking, so we don't know we're not really thinking, but feeling.

35.

We may feel we've got life all figured out because we aren't thinking, just feeling.

36.

We would give up a lesser pleasure for a greater one, but happiness is all the same.

37.

Pleasure is without happiness and happiness is without pleasure.

38.

We look out for desire, but we don't look out for ourselves because pleasure far outweighs the fear of pain.

39.
Pleasure is the result of desire. A lifetime of stress, anxiety and turmoil is all that's in between. Then, until we can see this, our lives are just in between.

40.
Happiness can last a lifetime, but pleasure is just temporary and must be reinforced for a lifetime.

41.
Pleasure does not want to know happiness and happiness does not want to know pleasure.

42.
Pleasure is a detriment to our health, well-being, happiness and wisdom.

43.
We confuse pleasure with happiness. That is why pleasure's authority over us is confusing. Just because something feels good, it may not be the best for us.

44.
We will relinquish authority over ourselves to what or who will give us more pleasure.

45.
Pleasure is no friend but just a hindrance to becoming happy. When we know this, we will know what to do at all times.

46.
We may never know the problem with life was us, because only a fool would try to tell someone something they don't want to know. Our greatest pleasures were the greatest control.

47.
When we limit our desires, we will maximize our freedom to be happy. We don't know this because pleasure rules the day and night too.

48.

We can't find our faults because we would have to be looking and there's no pleasure in that when pleasure is all we seek.

49.

We work so hard for so little pleasure that lasts for a while, without knowing we sacrificed our happiness.

50.

The inherent problem with pleasure is it only lasts for a short duration then must be reinforced again, and again, by doing over, and over. This isn't thinking.

51.

To own less is to in turn to own ourselves more because we can't own pleasure and be happy at the same time.

52.

Pleasure is a false positive. To possess is an act of being possessed.

53.

We are in a big hurry to have pleasure, but must slow down to have happiness.

54.

Due to our natural motivations, we will only seek pleasures without ever knowing what happiness even was.

55.

The desire for pleasure is always noticed because we strive for what is missing. Pleasure is always temporary. That's why it's always missing.

56.

We all can find pleasure, but very few are looking for happiness.

57.

If we are always trying to find out what gives us pleasure, there is no time left to be happy.

58.
If everyone is lost to the pursuit of pleasure, there is no one to keep score.

59.
To please others, we must consent to their wishes in the hopes of receiving pleasure in return, and also social stress, anxiety and despair (SAD).

60.
We are defined by our pleasures instead of happiness; that's not a deliberate life.

61.
Pleasure is in the absence of happiness and happiness is in the absence of pleasure.

62.
We feel that no time is being wasted in acquiring more for more's sake. There is never enough of what we don't need.

63.
If it looks, smells, sounds, tastes or feels good, don't do it because it is not good for us.

64.
We feel we know what pleasure is so we do not need to think.

65.
We must limit our pleasures in order to maximize our happiness, for what we own in turn owns us too.

66.
Desire for pleasure is addictive. That is why we can't get enough of what we don't need.

67.
All pleasure is a gift that keeps on taking mind's and body's pasts and futures that could have been a life of meaning.

68.
If it feels good it does not last.

69.
We have freedom to become happy, but we must pay to have all pleasures.

70.
Nobody wants to see us be happy because that doesn't give them any pleasure. Pleasure is with others and happiness is by ourselves.

71.
We could know what makes us happy, but we're too busy doing what gives us pleasure.

72.
We are willing to withstand hardship, adversity or stress for the pleasure of others.

73.
We may know what is good, but we rarely know what is good for us. That is the difference between pleasure and happiness.

74.
Pleasure is a false positive because it lacks reason of logic.

75.
Pleasure is at all costs.

76.
What we like is irrelevant to what is best for us.

77.
We can be happy alone or have pleasure with others.

78.
If all we want is pleasure, we wouldn't get anything else.

79.
Pleasure prevails even though it's not wise.

80.

We are up and we are down. Around and around we go. This is not as much fun as we felt it would be.

81.

We often are what we don't want to become. Beware of life's pleasures and fun.

82.

We seem not to want to know the truth if it does not make us feel good.

83.

We all know what we want is to have pleasure, but that is also the reason why we are not happy now.

84.

We can have pleasure, but we can't let pleasure have us at the loss of peace and calm.

85.

We don't desire wisdom or enlightenment because we aren't wise or enlightened, so we must desire pleasure because that's all we will ever get.

86.

All pleasures are knowing what our desires were. That's not thinking but feeling.

87.

Our pleasures can only happen at the cost of our happiness. That is our two mind's struggle to win again.

88.

We can't say we think if we desire pleasure instead.

89.

When we are always seeking pleasure, how would we ever know of anything else?

90.
All pleasures will lead to problems.

91.
If we get what we wanted, then desire for pleasure is all we have learned.

92.
We are seduced by our weaknesses and don't want to know anything else.

93.
When we think about it, pleasure is meaningless.

94.
Our influence over ourselves is for us, but power over others is pleasure.

95.
Take no pleasure or become a prisoner unto ourselves.

96.
"Have pleasure now and be happy later," is how we feel.

97.
Pleasure is power over us, but reason is influence over ourselves.

98.
No pleasure is actually worth the trouble to acquire.

99.
Passion speaks louder than our mind does.

100.
All pleasures subside, but happiness doesn't.

101.
The power of pleasure or the influence of happiness?

102.
We all may have what we wanted, but we don't like what we have become, because all pleasures are temporary.

103.
Although we are free to do as we please, this is what controls us the most.

104.
Pleasure isn't real because it's a self-induced, drugged fantasy.

105.
Pleasure has only brought me folly.

106.
Pleasure is the result of our desires for dopamine, a natural but outdated instinct that is not valid in our current society or higher mental ability.

107.
Do we have pleasure or does pleasure have us? Free will must become our will to be free.

108.
Pleasure rules us all from the most hidden regions of our minds.

109.
All we ever wanted was pleasure, but all we ever needed was happiness.

110.
We feel pleasure is worth anything, even risking all to get.

111.
We seek out the gates of servitude and it feels good to do as one pleases.

112.
Pleasure resents happiness because emotion resents thinking. One must die so the other may live.

113.
We are out of our minds with the desires for pleasures.

114.
Alienation increases with technology because pleasures are competing.

115.
We do not have pleasure because pleasure has us.

116.
It is more pleasurable to have fun with others than to be peaceful and calm.

117.
We are obsessed with what feels good.

118.
We like pleasure more than happiness because we do what we want to do and not what we need to do.

119.
When we are not thinking, but desiring pleasure, we don't know we're not thinking.

120.
Pleasure is always at the end of our tunnel vision because we have never considered happiness as an alternative.

121.
When we get what we wanted and are not happy very long, that is because we wanted pleasure and not happiness.

122.
Pleasure is never worth more than happiness. We won't know this if we are not the boss of ourselves.

123.
Pleasure doesn't make us happy, for more pleasure is less happiness.

124.
Pleasure, what we have to do to get and keep, is not worth a lifetime of stress, anxiety and despair. If we only thought, we would know this.

125.
We feel good if we get what we desire so that pleasure reinforces our motives without thinking.

126.
Emotion not reason is the same as pleasure not happiness.

127.
When we think about it, pleasure is too much trouble.

128.
Sadness is when we miss pleasure.

129.
We should not trust anything we feel because it's our worst friend and best enemy.

130.
Pleasure is not worth the pain.

131.
Being alone is happiness, but we will never know this if pleasure is our only motivation.

132.
We could use our thinking for happiness instead of just feeling pleasure.

133.
Pleasure costs money but happiness is free.

134.
We are in servitude by submission to desires when we do as we please.

135.
Pleasure is our enemy when we feel it's our friend.

136.
We have no idea why we do what we must do, except that it makes us feel good.

137.
We are possessed to possess possessions. Is that feeling or thinking?

138.
Pleasure is self-prophesizing.

139.
All we want is pleasure. That's our cause without any knowledge of control.

140.
Our lives are spent in the pursuit of pleasure, directly or indirectly.

141.
The uninformed would have nothing if they didn't have pleasure.

142.
Pleasure has to be reinforced again and again, while happiness can last.

143.
The less pleasure we have the happier we are.

144.
Mindless instincts are behind the obvious, so it's very hard to detect. Pleasure is in opposition to knowledge of our self.

145.
Doesn't everyone give pleasure in order to receive pleasure?

146.
Pleasure let me be. For we have a life we may never see.

147.
We may do things wrong when they feel so good.

148.
Pleasure and happiness are in sharp contrast. That's why life is in such a conflict.

149.
If we get what we want, we will be better, never seems to work.

150.
Happiness eludes us because we desire pleasure instead.

151.
Wishful thinking doesn't seem to work, but it is more pleasurable than reality.

152.
Postponed pleasures may be newfound freedom from our selves.

153.
What we must do for pleasure.

154.
When we love pleasure we cannot be happy.

155.
We like pleasure more than the pain we'll suffer; this is why we are not happy.

156.
We will do anything for pleasure except think.

157.
The pain we endure for the pleasure we desire, doesn't teach us to be happy if we don't learn.

158.
How could we ever improve our lives when we feel pleasure is all there is?

159.
We must beware of what gives us pleasure because it's a fantasy.

160.
Pleasure always wins when we desire without thinking.

161.
Pleasure is in the eye of the beholder, but not in their higher thinking.

162.
Since pleasure and fear are so easy to sell, then that must be our weakness.

163.
We have evolved from pleasure for pleasures without thinking.

164.
Quality of life is happiness, but quantity of possessions is pleasure.

165.
We all like pleasure, but it's not our friend because it limits our happiness.

166.
Emotions exclude a higher form of life.

167.
When we have money it is very pleasurable, but that's not happiness.

168.
Pleasure may be harmful to your health.

169.
Pleasure is without thinking and thinking is without pleasure.

170.
We defend our pleasure with our lives until our deaths.

171.
We thought we always knew what decisions to make. Well, we may never have considered they're emotions and not thinking.

172.
We like pleasure but pleasure doesn't like us.

173.
Pleasure or happiness, what requires the least amount of effort?

174.
Others are vexing for their authority is our pleasure.

175.
We must give up pleasure in order to have happiness because we are slaves to our wishes and desires—all emotions are motivations.

176.
We love intercourse because we wouldn't be here if we did not.

177.
We can see what is clear but ignore the rest.

178.
We are what we want to be, but we are also out of control of our mind, not our senses.

179.
When we flee pleasure we will find happiness.

180.
When pleasure is all we get it never lasts long enough.

181.
When we finally realize that pleasure only keeps us from happiness, what is there left for us to do?

182.
Of all the qualities we may have, we seem to only strive for pleasure and not happiness.

183.
Do we have pleasure or does pleasure have us?

184.
Pleasure is like a two pointed sword: a coercive power as an instrument of self-destruction.

185.
Pleasure is self-satisfaction accompanied by unawareness of actual deficiencies and dangers.

186.
Now is the culmination of our feelings or thinking.

187.
Pleasure is addictive; just look at us all helplessly awaiting for the next fix.

188.
Others may give us pleasure but only we can give ourselves happiness.

189.
Pleasure opposes happiness and happiness opposes pleasure all the days of our lives.

190.
We are bewildered by the promise of pleasure so as not to think clearly.

191.
We don't want to know what's best for us because it may distract from our pleasure.

192.
To be ignorant or a fool may give us pleasure, but without doubt we will not be happy.

193.
Pleasure or happiness: one may be false because they both can't be good for us.

194.
We have learned that society feels what is important is to have pleasure, or we could learn that what life teaches us is to be happy.

195.
We see only what promises to offer pleasure and will leave all the rest of life unknown.

196.
Desire is not the solution because pleasure is the problem.

197.
We may know others even more than we know ourselves because we get pleasure from others.

198.
We will trade reason or logic anytime for pleasure in our lives. This is the cause of our unhappiness.

199.
We are out of our minds for pleasure, but must go into our minds for happiness.

200.
We'll do anything we can to have pleasure, but we do nothing to become happy.

201.
Everybody knows what gives them pleasure; well that's also what limits our happiness too.

202.
There is opposition between pleasure and happiness; that nullifies happiness.

203.
We don't desire to be happy because it doesn't give us pleasure.

CHAPTER SIX

SOCIETY:
The effects of our dysfunction

1.
Society is the effect of our dysfunction by teaching us money and love is more valuable than anything, and not what happiness is.

2
We have accepted society's tendency for us to be governed by desire or fear without ever having thought anything about it.

3.
All life crashes down on us like a heavy surf. Then why do we insist on going into the water every day to work?

4.
We're all clustered together in cities and houses paying homage to our desires and fears while suffering all the stress, anxiety, and despair is the price we pay for our desire and fear.

5.
The lights of society shine much brighter than enlightenment ever will.

6.
Together in a society we have more fun and excitement, but alone in nature we have more peace and quiet.

7.
We must leave our cities for the simpler security of nature. That's the creative controlling force of happiness.

8.
We should not allow society to govern our thinking because that's not free thinking.

9.
Our societies become progressively dysfunctional as they progress away from the laws of nature, toward society's laws and values.

10.
We seek the respect of others, but lack the self-respect of ourselves.

11.
When we share our lives with others we lose our lives to them.

12.
Our will to be different than anyone else will result in a willingness to just be ourselves.

13.
Societies satisfy our weakness of ego, lust, fear (money, sex, time), but doesn't teach us that intelligence is not wisdom.

14.
We are trying to be just like everyone else but they're not happy either. What's wrong with them is also wrong with us.

15.
Our society of others, mates, careers and houses makes us slaves to our desires or prisoners of our fears.

16.
Up and up into our highest reaches as far as we can go is as far as we can reason. That's to be free from all that society teaches.

17.
We allow everyone and everything to detour us from ever thinking of a meaningful life.

18.
Our societies are the results of the laws of nature that's desire for pleasure and fear of pain. Our upper thinking is wisdom not foolishness.

19.
Happiness is not in demand without an option of free will.

20.
Our greatness isn't what others think about us; it lies in what we know of ourselves and life.

21.
We live in society because of our weaknesses and not our strengths. When we're controlled by our strengths, we must leave society.

22.
We are conceived and live in a system without any knowledge or regard for any other way of life.

23.
When our ends are frivolous then those means to the ends were frivolous.

24.
Bondage is our loss of courage.

25.
Some may tell us all they feel, but we won't know anymore.

26.
When we endeavor to be like everyone else, we will be like no one.

27.
When we felt we were so right, we were actually so wrong because we have been running in the wrong direction.

28.
We must become number one in our lives because our life is not for someone else's pleasure; in return or we will never become happy ourselves.

29.
We may have gotten more instructions on how a computer system functions than on how our brain systems function.

30.
Righteousness is the establishment of an authoritarian order that forces its beliefs and values on a less dominant person as a prerequisite for access, acceptance to that order.

31.
When we seek sameness we lose open-mindedness.

32.
When our higher thinking deviates from society's motivations for pleasure or fear, we are wiser.

33.
Our happiness is the effects of experiencing nature, but our pleasure is the effect of experiencing societies.

34.
Our experiences and not possessions are what enriches our mind's life, and not what others think about us.

35.
We must listen to the world around us and not artificial societies we made and occupy.

36.
Try harder to become different because sameness is just plain limiting.

37.
United we stand, divided we fall, so be at one within ourselves.

38.
We embrace our sameness for pleasure but not our differences for wisdom.

39.
Baggage is all we have.

40.
What we think of ourselves is far more important than what others think of us.

41.
We have the greatest reasons and definitions for success, but if we are wrong, our life is meaningless.

42.
We must be in a hurry to die, never to see life clearly.

43.
We choose to please others so as to please ourselves. We have to take time in order to have time for ourselves.

44.
If there is greatness within us, surely it's repressed by society's demands.

45.
Reality is from consciousness, experiences, reflection, and not society's opinion of itself.

46.
How can we think out of the box when it feels so good when we were in the box? We're boxed in by the pleasures of society.

47.
Undertaking responsibility by assuming obligations in order to be received favorably for the satisfaction of each other is mutual.

48.
Life's greatest value to us is in our experience and awareness and not in our accomplishments.

49.
If we weren't blinded by ourselves and others, we could become happy now.

50.
We have to think for ourselves or someone else will.

51.
Society rewards our desires for pleasures while satisfying our fears of the unknown.

52.
Society is a dumbing down because it's not relative to happiness at all.

53.
Money only satisfies our weaknesses not our strengths.

54.
Jobs, opportunities and sex are in the cities and where our desire for pleasure rules us all.

55.
If one mindedness is our education, doesn't that also close our minds to the truth of setting us free?

56.
Our desire to conform is for the pleasures of others and ourselves.

57.
When we are always in society, it limits our ability to think clearly. We are controlled by what controls us, that's not freedom from us.

58.
Societies are ego, lust, fear while nature is peace, joy, and happiness.

59.
All education is a belief in predestination, determinism for society's needs.

60.
Friendship is a favorable acceptance by granting approval to be used by both for mutual pleasure.

61.
We are eternally controlled by others because they give us what we desire or fear.

62.
Society creates dependency, but self-sufficiency is freedom.

63.
When we are always looking down at our lives daily demands we have created, we have to look up to see where we're going.

64.
The burden of supporting a greatly increased army and civil service taxed the resources of the people to a breaking point, people left the cities for the simpler security of the farm. (The Decline and Fall of the Roman Empire (337 to 476 AD)

65.
When we do what we see others do, we lie to ourselves.

66.
The oppression of our minds is weighted down by the apprehension of responsibilities.

67.
When we come under the spell of desire and fear, we need others and are thus dependent the rest of our days.

68.
When we do what others want of us, we are giving them pleasure in order for them to give us pleasure in return.

69.
Our life is better by figuring it out for ourselves. This is accomplished by varying degrees of success. We can learn by our mistakes, so make all the mistakes we can, but learn.

70.
We are controlled by others for their pleasures and ours also.

71.
All life's struggles are the will of others from ourselves, but until we know this we are not free or happy.

72.
Anything we own also owns us. From the desire to possess we will in turn be possessed.

73.
Those who work hard to acquire much always lose everything in the end.

74.
Our lives are filled with the necessities we feel are important, but feelings do not possess sound judgement.

75.
We are controlled by what controls us. Let that be nature for our happiness and not society for our pleasures. Isolation is an opportunity to know life not society.

76.
The work place is detrimental to our happiness, but not our desire for pleasures.

77.
Everyone wants us for the pleasures they can receive.

78.
We may not be capable of escaping the deceptions of society because desire has the power to deceive.

79.
The loss of courage is the loss of our freedom.

80.
We get approval of others by enduring others without thinking: to be regarded as proper in order to receive a favorable response or socially acceptable.

81.
We are searching for someone or something that will captivate and dominate by an irresistible desire for pleasure.

82.
Our weaknesses will defeat us, but our strengths will prevail.

83.
We are easily led by others in society to conform for our mutual pleasures and fears.

84.
Societies are like schools of fish. We will feel safer in numbers, but unlike schools of fish at greater risk.

85.
Truth is our ability to see ourselves clearly. That's indispensable to happiness, but truth collides with all society.

86.
Our bondage is not going the best way. It is going the way of our weaknesses.

87.
When we become an adult we are able to supply for ourselves. What society has taught us was how to struggle from irresistible forces.

88.
When pleasure and fear is the boss we will work for them at all costs. To become free, we must control what controls us, which is us.

89.
We must open our minds up to what's possible without the controls of others or ourselves.

90.
There has been little value placed on peaceful. So what's that worth?

91.
The greatest leaders must lead by example for our empowerment, and not as an enabler of our desires and fears.

92.
In society we are controlled by our mutual needs and not our wants in order to become happy.

93.
A self-made person is driven by ego, lust and fear.

94.
Wisdom is our isolation from others because we can't fight ignorance in society. We must flee to the simpler security of nature.

95.
To measure our life to any other would be self-limiting because all have missed the mark.

96.
Our uniqueness shouldn't require us to change, but society does for us to be accepted.

97.
When we give our lives to somebody else we are left without a life of our own.

98.
Money has no value except what society places on it because if we were the only person in the world money would have no value.

99.
Our group mentality is for mutual pleasure and is a form of dumbing down by societies.

100.
Societies are the effects of our desires and fears and not our happiness.

101.
All accomplishments are deemed by others values, not our own imaginations.

102.
The individual matters more than the community because if we are not happy the community has to be responsible.

103.

We can only have freedom in life from ourselves and not all the outside forces that control us.

104.

All societies are the effects of our emotional state of mind and not our higher thinking.

105.

The more money we make the more stress and anxiety we make.

106.

It is easier to cope with life than it is with society.

107.

Avoiding something desirable is the acknowledgment of one's own life and not that of others.

108.

Our conformity is the basis of our limitations.

109.

Money is our master from desire to fear.

110.

Society's rank and status results in fame and fortunes for our breeding and pleasure.

111.

Our desires and fears compel us to be at one with society for our sameness.

112.

We must know the difference in order to become different.

113.

Happiness is withdrawal from society to a quiet, peaceful secure life in nature.

114.
Society resonates with our desires, but nature resonates with our thinking.

115.
There is no satisfaction with possessions or status in society when we feel more is better.

116.
We are living our self-inflicted life from what others will think about us.

117.
To be normal is not good enough because average is dysfunctional; we just have to look all around us for the proof.

118.
We yield ourselves to the authorities of another for our mutual pleasure or fears. To become free we must have control of our own thinking and not that of others.

119.
We must see ahead in order to rise up or we will just fall down when we look down.

120.
We can give and give forever, but that only takes away from us.

121.
Mind sets are self-limiting while open minds are self-rewarding.

122.
Simply unaffected is our original state and without society we are free to be ourselves.

123.
If a child knows desire and fear, have adults learned nothing but just more of the same?

124.
We can't think clearly when we are with others.

125.
We rule or are ruled by decisions of domination.

126.
When our greatest resolve is driven by our lowest feelings, they are unrealized until we become the driver and not others.

127.
Ownership is self-induced slavery to our ego, lust and fear.

128.
Let us be ourselves to the height our mind can reach and not the depths of our fears or desires.

129.
It is not easy to think for ourselves when everyone else does it for us and our body has a mind of its own.

130.
We are not unique when we simply think like everyone else. We are just self-limiting.

131.
When we are taken in by the authority of others or possessions, we are permanently fixed to the ties that bind us all together.

132.
We may judge too simply when we don't even know what success is.

133.
It's easier to be unique than it is to conform.

134.
Education is no substitute for experience.

135.
We give authority over us to others for their own purposes.

136.
We must free ourselves for no one else has the knowledge, power or will except only to enslave.

137.
We sell our lives for money.

138.
Conformity to societies and their educational system rewards our desires and fears.

139.
Our value systems are instinctually based on emotions, not reasoned out. Our instincts are in our times today. That means if it feels good we do it. This also is harmful in its own way.

140.
To yield to the authority, the will of another, for the exchange of mutual pleasure or anticipated fear is our instinctual reality.

141.
We are always managed defensively when we're out of control.

142.
We can do anything we want but deserve just what we get by the laws of nature and society.

143.
No one can walk our mile in place of us, otherwise we would only learn what we are told.

144.
We have learned what we were taught, whether that's good or bad.

145.
We are slaves to the wishes and desires of others without ever knowing. There is little we do without the approval of others.

146.
Society gives us pleasure while nature gives us happiness.

147.
We do what others want us to do, to be accepted.

148.
Jobs are self-imposed slavery to our desires and fears instinctively.

149.
We can see that as a society gets older its government gets more personally restrictive.

150.
Society gives us pleasures in exchange for stress and anxiety. Nature gives us happiness in exchange for peace and tranquility.

151.
Might is right in nature, but right is might in society.

152.
Society is our subjection to the will of others for ours and their own desires and fears.

153.
When our mind is set we won't learn new experiences.

154.
To cast off social restraint, attitudes causing anxiety or suspicion, this accompanies our desires and fears.

155.
We all seem to seek the sameness of others. That makes us compatible but also disturbs internal calm that frees us from turmoil.

156.
When we have a strong want to be fulfilled it is without thinking on our own, but society.

157.
Our intelligence is artificially induced by society's determinism called education or self-driven education.

158.
To leave society and embrace nature is our higher thinking.

159.
When we don't strive for fame or fortune, we are free to seek what benefits us as a whole and not for a part of ourselves.

160.
Our societies are the effects of our desires for pleasure and fear of pain.

161.
We serve the needs of others by serving the needs of ourselves.

162.
When we desire pleasure it produces stress, anxiety and despair. That's found with others in cities.

163.
To just be ourselves we cannot be for someone else.

164.
Everyone wants us for the pleasures derived; that's life from emotions but not thinking.

165.
We are the results of our heredity and environment; that's the education of our societies.

166.
If our intelligence is a pretense, then it's just for our popularity.

167.
Intelligence can result in our infatuation with the messenger and not the message.

168.
Society is the extension of our minds desires and fears, so this is why it is dysfunctional to be happy for quality of life and peace of mind.

169.
Our problems in society are the effects of our natural instincts.

170.
Society's rewards are pleasurable, but we have to sacrifice our higher thinking in order to qualify.

171.
When we are always running around it's hard to know ourselves or life.

172.
The knowledge we acquire in society will not make us happy.

173.
Our successes will lead to our failure.

174.
When wisdom is acquired, society's motivations are unwise.

175.
True greatness will come from the opinions of others and not from the opinions of ourselves.

176.
Societies enable our desires and fears so we'll have to teach ourselves how to be happy.

177.
We will be ruled by others until we become rulers of ourselves.

178.
Social degradation is associated with working solely at the bidding of mutual desires and fears.

179.
To be alone in nature for long periods of time is very peaceful and humbling so few will know life beyond the distractions of society.

180.
We are so intent on walking in the ways of others we lose our own way.

181.
When we get what we sought we will have learned of our folly.

182.
Maybe it's better not to follow others but better to lead ourselves.

183.
Our dependence on others' impressions will also make us slaves to their desires and fears.

184.
We are either leaders or followers of others, or we must lead ourselves to not be misled.

185.
Our inner tranquility will be lost to our outer effectiveness.

186.
We are compelled to seek more for others' respect and feel we can never get enough.

187.
We may desire to be like everyone else but that will not show us how to become free.

188.
The easiest way is in nature but the hardest way is in society.

189.
All that we acquired in our life is going to be unnecessary baggage until we realize it is meaningless.

190.
We are finally grown up when all the problems that govern societies doesn't govern us any longer.

CHAPTER SEVEN

NATURE:
All is by the laws of nature

1.
We get what we deserve without question, but what we might not know is it was by the laws of nature.

2.
When we think about it our happiness is peace, quiet, tranquility and harmony that's found by being alone in nature.

3.
Social withdrawal from our pleasures of others is our happiness in nature, free from ourselves.

4
Our lives are imperfectly conceived or not very well thought out. That's nature's purposely concealed attempt to confuse and evade knowledge of ourselves because it's not fun.

5.
The happiest days of our life will be in the presence of nature, for only being alone in nature is real.

6.
Does life do us or do we do life? We would need to know our nature before we can live life to the fullest.

7.
Our power over others for pleasure is not a life but just an appendage to nature's instincts.

8.

The people come and must go but few will comprehend that all suffering was nature's own making.

9.

The withdrawal from society to live in the simpler security of a natural life in nature is peaceful and calm.

10.

Societies can give us the desires we want but in nature we will receive peace from ourselves.

11.

Pleasure is nature's way of getting us to do something we would not do if we thought about it.

12.

We are driven by nature's will that runs through us without knowing it's not our own. We are all so full of nature's instincts without ever really knowing ourselves.

13.

Nature is a simpler mode of life resembling liberty, abundance and generosity.

14.

Nature's instinctive value system is based on desire and maintained by us not thinking.

15.

We are the effects of nature's causes in us or our own causes over nature.

16.

Aren't life's problems due to nature's instinctive motivations that control our lives?

17.

We are the results of nature that created us, but it is most difficult to alter those effects. It is a caste system that limits us without us even knowing.

18.
We know where our 'on' button is but not where our 'off' button is.

19.
Our world is a reflection of human nature but our lives could become an introspection. This would be our higher thinking over the dictates of nature.

20.
Life is the consciousness of nature's effects.

21.
Our experience in life is the effects of nature's instincts until we think and not feel.

22.
In our societies we are separated from nature.

23.
Our life is not about us, for nature runs its course through every thought we ever have.

24.
The closer to nature the closer to heaven. We've just got to think about that.

25.
Nature is the highest order of life but the lowest order of our thinking.

26.
Beauty is nature's way of attracting. We cannot resist in its many ways.

27.
We can live a life of more peace, joy and happiness alone in nature.

28.
Nature is killing us with our own desires and fears because we're not thinking.

29.
Nature is very entertaining without seeking anything else.

30.
Nature nurtures our happiness.

31.
Nature is also a minimalist.

32.
Life glorifies life by its existence.

33.
Life breaks the wrong and makes the strong.

34.
Life is our discovery of nature, society and ourselves.

35.
All life is driven by forces unknown to itself.

36.
Nature's motivations clearly run its course through us without our knowing.

37.
We are but an appendage of nature's motivations.

38.
All the demands of nature are our nature.

39.
Nature made us and will also destroy us very soon in the end.

40.
Nature's motivations rule the unwise and unenlightened with a strong force.

41.
Human emotions have perpetuated our species and will surely destroy us all in the end.

42.
We will suffer the dictates of nature's rules over us because we felt our choices were free will.

43.
We are given life and death in equal proportions by nature's plans.

44.
Nature runs its course throughout all life without life ever knowing.

45.
In nature's laws there is no good or bad but we judge them on how they affect our lives.

46.
The desires for pleasure resulted in global warming and the fears of pain resulted in atomic weapons, for all nature's master plan is for life's extinction.

47.
We are ruled by allowing nature to take its course or we may rule our own course.

48.
Nature is like the mother of the house and will also kick us all out of the house in the end.

49.
When we're alive we're living on top of nature but when we die we've just moved inside of nature.

50.
The motivations of nature are desirable for sure but ultimately detrimental to our health, happiness, and longevity of the human race.

51.
Fools know they're fooling around.

52.
We are lost without thinking, so we are lost.

CHAPTER EIGHT

TRUTH:
Always fallen on deaf ears

1.
Nothing more can be said because we must not even want to hear, for the truth has always fallen on deaf ears.

2.
Our truth is the ability to know that the cause of our discontent was us.

3.
There is a credibility gap between what we feel and what is real.

4.
The way to not know the truth is by our enemy's emotions.

5.
When we lie, cheat or steal we will rob ourselves of respect, dignity and confidence.

6.
Success is found by influencing ourselves and not in power over each other.

7.
The greatest secret of our lives is that we are our worst enemy and don't even know it.

8.
Life is much easier to be deceived than it is to be perceived.

9.
We may have problems in life but they're usually within us, which is why we haven't figured them out yet.

10.
If the mind preceded our actions then therein lays the problems of the human race.

11.
Slavery is from desires and fears. Freedom is from reason and logic.

12.
Our will is from emotions and feelings or reason and logic.

13.
We are challenged more by ourselves than by life's necessities, of food and shelter.

14.
We may be over opinionated for our abilities.

15.
We don't want to know life if it is different than what we feel.

16.
Our quality of life isn't a factor in the quantity of our life styles.

17.
Our lives will become as full as they can when we think clearly because that's the law of reality as opposed to appearance.

18.
Life is fair; we are not to expect anything other than the truth. We may not be capable.

19.
Nature is absolute truth.

20.
We can't serve two masters at the same time: emotions or truth.

21.
We mistake the truth for the things we want to feel.

22.
We are governed by our weaknesses or liberated by our strengths.

23.
The more we give up, the more we will have because truth is often the opposite of what we may feel.

24.
Let there be light into the darkest depths of our minds for truth will set us free from ourselves and others.

25.
We have our life's motivations at birth with just the details of our living it out at the whims of time and change.

26.
Dysfunctional is our inability to cope with ourselves, not life, because all life is as it should be.

27.
We are always trying to conquer others. Maybe we should be trying to conquer ourselves first.

28.
We all deserve who we have become, but in most cases that may not be good.

29.
We are either a victim of our instinctual feelings or a victor over them.

30.
It seems to be easier to be honest to others than it is to be honest to ourselves.

31.
The past is our limitations for the future. Without knowing this we are locked in the present situations all our lives.

32.
We do anything we want and deserve exactly what we get. Isn't that sublime?

33.
Our highest mental capacity is circumvented by our lowest ability to think clearly. We are controlled by our weaknesses and not by our strengths.

34.
The truth is hard to find when we're not looking.

35.
We are always driven by the same forces without knowing ourselves.

36.
We want all things except any regulation of ourselves for the sake of improvement.

37.
Maybe we only know as much as we desire to know.

38.
We may not see who we really are because we never looked.

39.
When life seems more trouble than it is worth we would have to admit we are doing something wrong.

40.
We can't add to or subtract from absolute truth.

41.
Life's not broken; we need to fix ourselves.

42.
Our presence of mind or presence of feelings is our honesty or dishonesty to ourselves.

43.

We are wrong when we feel we are right, or we are right when we feel we are wrong?

44.

A lie to anyone is a lie to ourselves, for who we could have been and not as we are now.

45.

When life is the best it can be then we should be too.

46.

When we don't listen we don't learn.

47.

We are always on a treadmill of our own making.

48.

The body pulls the mind or the mind pulls the body. The results are we will suffer or not.

49.

Our death is in accordance with all of life's end results. When we accept truth as a real event is the final state of our affairs we can understand life.

50.

We are out of control most when we feel we are in control.

51.

All life is consuming or is consumed by life.

52.

Truth is not pleasure but happiness.

53.

We are a burden unto ourselves until we know this.

54.

Our past was in hopes of just a good time but our futures are in hopes of just more time.

55.
There is no joy in reason.

56.
We will thrive on the truth, but will die on the lies.

57.
Happiness is the result of truth.

58.
The truth doesn't need to ever defend itself once it has been stated.

59.
Because we are the product of our feelings it has been a good or bad effect on our lives. We can have no defense.

60.
There are many who wish to have power over our minds and hearts. Only through our experiences and reflection will come unabridged truth.

61.
We will become what we are thinking about.

62.
We can keep our minds on what's meaningful by using our common sense.

63.
We must stop what we're feeling because it's not working very well.

64.
When we don't question, we won't know.

65.
When we are wrong we didn't know right and it hurts, that is how we know we must learn.

66.
We have a strong aversion to the truth if it isn't desirable.

67.
Life is hard work if we do not know any better.

68.
Some day we will disappear just like we were never here.

69.
We can't trust most people's opinion when they're limited by their emotions.

70.
There is a credibility gap if life is good and we are not.

71.
We must consume life in order to live.

72.
We are the most sure of ourselves when we're most wrong.

73.
Reason is the source of absolute truth that resonates with experience for our highest knowledge,
influence, and will.

74.
Wouldn't sound prudent judgement promote quiet, calm results as a self-evident truth?

75.
We seem to be searching for something different again and again. It's just the same things but we expected different results.

76.
We are the problem until we become the solution.

77.
We must visualize ourselves as we are going to become and not as we are now.

78.
Our emotions own us or we own our emotions.

79.
This is who we are by doing what we are doing.

80.
We may feel we have life figured out when we don't.

81.
We are defined by the chances we take and the limitations of our minds and bodies.

82.
Anybody can write a book but few can write a meaningful book.

83.
There is no good death, for it is all the same.

84.
Life is best measured by our experiences and not the possessions acquired along the way.

85.
What we don't know is more important than what we do know if we don't know ourselves.

86.
Shouldn't our highest objective be to become aware of problems we caused to ourselves?

87.
To know why we are suffering in our life is just to know ourselves.

88.
We are judged by fools, but not by the wise.

89.
When all we want to know is what we desire, it is self-limiting.

90.
We are the beast within us; with this awareness we can become free.

91.
It would take a lifetime to alter what we have been taught, but that's if we're trying.

92.
We have avoided knowing ourselves long enough.

93.
Life is good no matter where you are at in life.

94.
To know one subject better than anything else, let it be us.

95.
The Ancient Greek aphorism "man, know thyself" has always fallen on deaf ears.

96.
How we improve our lives is how we improve ourselves.

97.
Don't acquire something if you don't want it to own you.

98.
We'll see farther if we think to look.

99.
We may not want to know the truth if it differs from what we desire or fear.

100.
Truth is reasoning over the illusion of our emotions.

101.
We may not cope with life very well without knowledge of the beast within us.

102.
We are defined by our weaknesses more than by our strengths.

103.
What we have acquired is meaningless if we are not peaceful, calm, tranquil, blissful, or harmonious.

104.
The package may be alluring, but the contents will be troubling.

105.
We are what we wanted to be, but not what we needed to become happy.

106.
We are the masters of our fate or fate was the master of us.

107.
We may surely come to life's end without ever knowing ourselves.

108.
We haven't found ourselves because we never looked.

109.
Within all success lays the burdens of that success.

110.
The real essence of anything is how we are affected, either positively or negatively.

111.
When we live in fear we will die in vain.

112.
All that we own is a fantasy we have paid our whole lives for in the end.

113.
Goodness comes to good people and badness comes to bad people, this is how we learn or not learn.

114.
The truth may not be desirable because all it has to be is the truth.

115.
We can overcome the strong by respect, for that's all they seek and this shows our greatness.

116.
When we oppose others they will oppose us, but when we are kind to others they are kind to us.

117.
The truth is also sound judgment while what we desire maybe wishful thinking.

118.
A life without flexibility is a life at risk.

119.
Our discipline will know life, liberty and the pursuit of happiness, but undisciplined will know death, bondage and the pursuit of desire.

120.
Nothing is possible without knowing what's impossible first.

121.
The limits we place on ourselves we do without thinking.

122.
When we talk we don't listen, when we don't listen we don't learn and when we don't learn we don't know.

123.
Why are the hardest things seen as valuable and the easiest things seen as invaluable?

124.
When we feel the most sure of our course in life beware: feelings are not thinking.

125.
There is nothing in life that's eternal except death.

126.
It is good to be good, but it's bad to be bad. There are some who don't know that yet.

127.
We are an adult in life or remain a child in life, a choice we all have made.

128.
We are internally conquered by all our conquests and in the end subdued by what we subdued.

129.
All truths are priceless but possessions are costly in time, honor and contentment.

130.
Small minds think big but big minds think small.

131.
The human race tends to rely on emotions as opposed to reason, resulting in pleasure and not happiness.

132.
Nature's truth is all around us but we would have to think to find it.

133.
When all we want to know is what we desire to know, that's very limited, don't you think?

134.
We are most sure of ourselves when we are actually the emptiest.

135.
Come up to this moment or let it slip by again.

136.
The meek shall inherit themselves through introspection.

137.
Life's greatest and hidden unknown is itself.

138.
There is no hope without will and there is no will without hope.

CHAPTER NINE

AWARENESS:
Life's accomplishment is awareness

1.
The proof of a person's life accomplishments is the awareness of our inward state and outward facts of life.

2.
To be aware of the unknown is to be aware of ourselves.

3.
We seem to be more aware of our bodies than we are of our minds.

4.
Our wisdom is functional before our awareness of it.

5.
All that is missing in our life is awareness that there is nothing missing in life.

6.
Now is the best time of our life to the degree of our awareness.

7.
We would actually have to see we are our own problem before the solution could ever become clear.

8.
The awareness of our higher thinking is required in order to become conscious of ourselves and all life.

9.
Self-bondage was our choice, but not self-awareness.

10.
Once we comprehend our limitations, we are capable of comprehending our strengths.

11.
We may never know ourselves without becoming aware of our thinking.

12.
Our lives will reflect non-thinking before awareness.

13.
Being without mental awareness is not readily seen. That's hiding life's secret defects from our full knowledge of those imperfections.

14.
We are very aware of the moment time seems to become special and not a burden we must deal with because of a dilemma we have created for ourselves.

15.
Through reflection and contemplation of our intentions we will acquire an awareness of reality.

16.
We must become aware of our limitations in order not to be limited.

17.
Maybe we are to blame for all our suffering because we have done everything we wanted.

18.
Awareness of our mental life is most important after life itself.

19.
A choice is ours once we can acquire self-awareness of one's own bodily functions.

20.
Beware of what's confining in order to become self-aware.

21.
To become aware of our unawareness is to turn the light upon us, and when we like what we see we have happiness and enlightenment.

22.
The self-awareness of one's individual personality, independent of outside stimulus, is without selfish desires for our satisfaction.

23.
We must become aware of our emotions so as to be cautious of our decisions.

24.
Once we have discovered our happiness, no amount of pleasure could change a mind that is aware.

25.
We won't see ourselves clearly when we haven't looked.

26.
We will not know ourselves when we are always looking for someone else.

27.
Beware of what we feel we want because in our conceit lies our defeat.

28.
When we possess something, aren't we in turn possessed by that same thing?

29.
Life is so good, but we are so far from that awareness. We must be going the wrong way to see life clearly.

30.
We have everything in order to be happy except awareness.

31.
Do we own our life or does our life own us? Do we control our minds or do our minds control us?

32.
Our professed, rather than real, purpose is to deceive ourselves.

33.
Life's goal is to get more when it should be a goal to know why we want more just for more's sake.

34.
The world seems to be against us but we still can't understand we are in conflict with our own best interests.

35.
The first thing we should know is that we don't know, but we don't know what we don't know yet.

36.
We would have to suspect we are limited before knowing limitations are real, for ignorance is a lack of knowledge because of ignorance.

37.
The only problems we have are the problems we have created ourselves.

38.
We come up to a wall all our lives, but cannot look over our limitations, for its not going to be easy. That is what's controlling us now.

39.
Stubborn is what got everyone where they are at now.

40.
To be aware of our awareness is a deliberate life.

41.
Our mind's eye may see before we are aware.

42.
If our minds are a mystery, then surely our lives must be a tragedy.

43.
We don't know everything just because we know what we want.

44.
What we do not know will hurt us.

45.
We don't have to deal with anybody but ourselves, so we're the problem.

46.
If we want to be better then we must not be ourselves.

47.
Our consciousness was always within us, but our awareness is deliberate for we can't think clearly and desire at the same.

48.
We must become aware of ourselves for a higher level of thinking to protect us.

49.
Pleasure is harming us, but we can't see because we're having fun because of stress, anxiety, and despair. This awareness will set us free.

50.
To acknowledge our anxiety, fear is self-awareness.

51.
We can become interested in our mental state of awareness for peace of mind.

52.
The inward state or awareness is our mind's ability as contrasted with life's unconscious processes that nature forces upon us.

53.
We can be in a bad place or we can come from a bad place.

54.
We travel the world to see other people so as not to see ourselves.

55.
Our field of view is self-limited.

56.
Our problem is: How are we supposed to learn to change?

57.
All our struggles in life are always with us.

58.
The only thing wrong with life is our opinion of it.

59.
We have to be incompatible with our senses in order to become well adjusted.

60.
We can get used to anything, but maybe we should not want to.

61.
So much stimuli is stimulating our mind's abilities to think clearly, and so much depression is depressing our mind's ability to think clearly.

62.
We are a detriment to ourselves without knowing it.

63.
We are helpless, but don't know it.

64.
We have been operating our minds all our lives without any instructions, no wonder we have some problems.

65.
Our lives are the results of our imagination or lack of the knowledge of that fact.

66.
When our decisions are for what feels good it's not thinking.

67.
It is difficult to gain new insight when we are predisposed by ownership or our old ideas.

68.
We are what we wanted but don't know it.

69.
Life runs its course through us every moment of our life without us really realizing we are not free.

70.
We have so much, but feel we have so little.

71.
We have two minds for motivation. One is for fun and the other is for real.

72.
If we don't look we won't see.

73.
We need to nullify our emotions in order to maximize our lives.

74.
We must need to see the extreme differences in life in order to find the best path.

75.
Our problems are cause to reflect on our lack of a solution.

76.
How could we possibly be right when we are so impossibly wrong?

77.
When we can't help ourselves, nobody will help us.

78.
Why is it so easy to see what we don't have, but it's so hard to see what we do have?

79.
In the end we all have to deal with our own anger and not someone else's or it will go on.

80.
Everything we have acquired will eventually have to be gotten rid of so why did we feel it was so important?

81.
The harm we do to ourselves is unrealized, so unmeasurable.

82.
We would have to know better in order to be better because more is not better.

83.
Just as soon as we feel we know what we want, we have also stopped thinking but have closed our minds.

84.
The gift of discovery not sought after is one's own capabilities, character, feelings and motivations.

85.
Our minds are the difference between good and bad in our lives.

86.
Life is just different times for different people, but the same motivations of life.

87.
We do what we want but not what we need.

88.
Our lives are overbearing because we let them be so.

89.
Since we're all doing what we wanted, then that is what's wrong with our lives?

90.
We need to progress past our incompetence because our incompetence is keeping us from progress.

91.
We must catch on in order to let go. For all life comes and goes without us ever really thinking. Our mind is a toy we must play with it for a discovery of our awareness.

92.
We are at war within ourselves because our discomfort was self-generated. That should have taught us but it hasn't.

93.
To become fully aware of life we must heighten our understanding and admiration.

94.
Attachment is slavery to our weaknesses.

95.
We are too busy doing what we have to do, but we are not too busy when we are doing what we want to do.

96.
If we don't know then we can't understand.

97.
Life is so good; why don't we know this when we do it our way all the time?

98.
What's in the belly of our beast that restricts our awareness of ourselves?

99.
Ego restricts self-awareness.

100.
That we don't know ourselves is the reason why we're unhappy.

101.
We feel we know, but that's not thinking.

102.
We don't know what we don't like to know will limit our knowledge.

103.
We seek to know all things outside of us, but few seek to know themselves so as to know the causes of their misfortunes.

104.
We have to know what's meaningless before we can know what's meaningful.

105.
All we may know is to understand less.

106.
We are chosen for consciousness by our awareness.

107.
We either feel or think and the results are going to be our lives.

108.
When the end of our lives is near, life seems so much more precious.

109.
Without knowing our limitations we will always remain limited.

110.
Life is not as important where we're at now, but where our minds are at now.

111.
We are defeated by our lack of the knowledge of nature.

112.
Our lives will improve by the degree of authority we have over our instinctive motivations.

113.
Retirement from work is a way to happiness or disaster; all is not as we may have perceived it to be.

114.
Time will disturb or soothes will show us our two minds workings.

115.
What's wrong with us is what's wrong with life.

116.
A companion is to live with and serve, but companionship is mutual interest.

117.
Life's contentment or contentiousness is how our two minds function.

118.
The worthiest goals are the easiest to attain, while the least worthy goals are the hardest to attain.

119.
As we concentrate our attention on profits and losses our lives are slipping away.

120.
When others' anger is returned with kindness they have no defense.

121.
Our deeds may not always match our needs.

122.
Our awareness is the knowledge of ignorance and may be the greatest quest of all.

123.
We will either honor ourselves or we will abuse ourselves, this is a no-brainer for sure.

124.
To understand our enemy is to know ourselves intimately.

125.
We will simplify our lives when we know that everybody wants something.

126.
When fame or fortune is respected more than anything else you are or will be unhappy.

127.
Without substance all and everything will rush in to fill our lives.

128.
When we are disadvantaged we will seek the advantages of wealth or happiness.

129.
Wisdom is born out of awareness when the pretense of desire ends.

130.
We are dysfunctional at knowing our motivations are harmful because we are in hopes of receiving pleasure instead of reason or logic.

131.
We will not be in danger when we're distrustful of our motivations.

132.
We are compelled through our lives, unaware of awareness till the end of time.

133.
We must know of our problems first in order to know of our solutions.

CHAPTER TEN

CONSCIOUSNESS AND CONSCIENCE:
Life's within our consciousness

1.
We are driven by our weaknesses, but we are the driver of our strengths. The difference lies within our consciousness.

2.
Be conscious of every moment. All life is made up of moments.

3.
Our consciousness will result in a higher quality of life, but our unconsciousness is a higher standard of living that's pleasurable.

4.
Banish the thought that separates conscience from consciousness.

5.
When our conscience is in harmony with our consciousness we are at peace.

6.
Our state of mind that's independent of consciousness is just existence.

7.
Our consciousness of life and ourselves is life's greatest accomplishment, coupled with the will to direct us to a higher form of our life.

8.
Life shouldn't be measured in our accomplishments, but the degree of consciousness.

9.
A meaningful life is measured by consciousness, but a meaningless life is measured by unconsciousness.

10.
There is in our minds a small entity that is of the greatest effect of our lives. That is our consciousness, conscience.

11.
Self-evident truths occur when consciousness reflects on experience.

12.
We are like icebergs where 10% is consciously seen and 90% is unconsciously unseen and unknown.

13.
There is a fine line between consciousness and unconsciousness, but a world of difference.

14.
We are not suspecting an enemy is within us all our lives, compelling our thoughts and actions without our consciousness.

15.
All of life is but a distraction from the meaningfulness that's within our minds and what's the most important is our consciousness of life's essence.

16.
What we do not know is causing us anguish.

17.
Our intelligence is used either to impress others for pleasure or to acquire consciousness for our happiness.

18.
To have lived and lost everything was inevitable, but to have acquired consciousness in our lives was divine.

19.
When we are conscious of life, it's everything; but when we are unconscious of life we want everything.

20.
We're the results of our distractions and not our concentration.

21.
Our conscience is like a spider in our mind just waiting for an unsuspecting mistake so as to come down and eat us alive, it's unforgiving and relentless.

22.
Our motivations are before our consciousness of those motivations.

23.
Raise our consciousness to know our unconsciousness.

24.
We are affected most by what's unconscious to us, but when we become conscious we can affect a state of influence over our own essence.

25.
Peace of mind is just our consciousness of what we have and not what we want.

26.
Our outward happiness is from our inward approval of our conscience.

27.
We must conform for pleasure or inform for happiness while one is pride of ownership, the other is empowerment of our consciousness.

28.
The cause of our freedom is consciousness and its effects are for our happiness, and a fear of desire for pleasure.

29.
We give up happiness for our own desires and fears. Through our consciousness we will know the differences.

30.
Our greatest consciousness is to know we are in heaven now.

31.
Our conscience will never regret being a good person.

32.
By always avoiding what we don't know is self-limiting.

33.
We are driven by the driver of our unconsciousness. Good luck because that's what we are going to need. Without consciousness we are surely destined to a life of suffering fear and desires.

34.
Our greatness will come from our greater consciousness.

35.
Our consciousness knows that feelings are counter to thinking.

36.
We can live our lives by choice or necessity.

37.
We must shed the old to have the new.

38.
We are like an empty vessel. Through consciousness or unconsciousness of what we put in our mouths and minds, we will become happy or unhappy.

39.
We need to protect us from ourselves, because to know our enemy is to know us.

40.
Mankind seems to be most flawed in our ability to view ourselves objectively.

41.
We have to become receptive to becoming conscious of ourselves in order to see life clearly.

42.
Without any doubt, we can never be sure of knowing.

43.
Unconsciousness is where we are all going without our knowing.

44.
We don't have time to become conscious of ourselves or life. Whose fault was that?

45.
We could run our lives, but our lives run us on an unconscious level by our feelings.

46.
Our free will is an illusion to our conscious mind.

47.
Through consciousness our imaginations can visualize opportunity.

48.
What was lost is found when we look around.

49.
Once we are conscious then we own that knowledge.

50.
Life interferes with our thinking or we would be better than we are.

51.
To be unconscious is a waste of time.

52.
Our life is good or bad from our thinking or lack of same. Let our conscience be our guide, or we must live by the consequences.

53.
When we are asleep, our minds know desire and fear; but when we are awakened, we can become conscious of ourselves and life.

54.

There is great insight within our consciousness; to know this we can be happy.

55.

Our consciousness of others distress is empathy, but wisdom is consciousness of ourselves. It comes from our distress or just more distress; it all was our life's choices.

56.

Conscious of consciousness is its own reward.

57.

We can know our unknown self.

58.

We make our own problems because we don't realize we are the problem.

59.

We detract from the quality of life.

60.

Looking at the moon is like looking at ourselves, familiar yet distant.

61.

We are either a victim or a victor of our conscience.

62.

We must see our past clearly in order to see where we are now.

63.

Ignorance doesn't know it is limited.

64.

If we regard ourselves with respect from an opinion obtained by reflection, it refreshes our mind.

65.

Our first thoughts are without thinking, but we won't know this if we don't actually question ourselves again and again.

66.
Why is life so good? We don't know because we have not really ever thought about it.

67.
We can foresee our failures when we think about our motivations.

68.
Thinking is consciousness.

69.
A life without consciousness is life-less.

70.
We must rise to the challenge or fall by the wayside like everyone else.

71.
Our conscience makes a better friend than it does an enemy; like trying to live with a contentious person.

72.
Life doesn't get us down because we do it to ourselves.

73.
A conscious life is the greatest appreciation of life's experience.

74.
It is very sad what we do to ourselves and then not learn from the mistakes we are making.

75.
Let us be more aware of our conscious reasoning as opposed to our unconscious emotions.

76.
When we can acknowledge our death we can acknowledge our lives more.

77.
To go or to stay will be determined by feelings or thinking.

78.
We are the master of others or the master of ourselves for we cannot serve two masters.

79.
There is no credibility gap between our life choices and our life.

80.
When the battle is over we will have beaten ourselves.

81.
When a person knows no limits they're not the boss of themselves.

82.
The contented have learned from all their disappointments but the not contented have not.

83.
All of the gains we have worked so hard for in life were also the loss of a real life that could have been.

84.
When our higher thinking knows our lower thinking we will know freedom.

85.
Thinking is more important than not thinking wouldn't you say?

86.
Thinking is our highest accomplishment but least used for our benefit.

87.
There is much more accomplished by thinking than by feeling.

88.
Those who think for themselves are free to think for themselves.

CHAPTER ELEVEN

HIGHER THINKING:
The degree of our happiness

1.
Our experiences in life are the effects of the mind's ability to know and direct itself. According to our higher thinking this will be the degree of our happiness.

2.
We are led by our emotions or we lead by our thinking.

3.
Our minds seem to be in the service of something else other than our own wellbeing.

4.
When we are in the presence of our higher thinking it feels like home. We will know this when we get there.

5.
Our desires are laboring, but our thinking is liberating. The difference is in our ability to comprehend ourselves.

6.
Our higher thinking is to become free from our desires and fears so we may be happy all the remaining days of our life.

7.
Our desires and fears are bondage to our instinctive emotions without the freedom of our higher thinking.

8.
We must serve our senses or we are in turn served by our higher thinking.

9.
We are all the prisoners of our mind's emotions or freed by our thinking.

10.
The more effort will not be a greater reward as we might feel, but it is actually just the opposite when we think.

11.
Our impulses are self-deceptive concerning facts and situations, leading to a disordered state of our higher thinking that's not present in our life.

12.
Nothing is more important in life than peace and quiet. If that's the last thing on our list it shows we may not be thinking.

13.
We can't have both pleasure and happiness. The course that is best or worst for us will be decided by either what we feel or think.

14.
We serve two masters, one is our body and the other is our mind. The results are quite different, but we are unlikely to know those differences without thinking.

15.
There is a union of our lower and higher thinking when the lower thinking finally acknowledges our higher thinking is best for both of us.

16.
If we ever stopped to think, desire and fear are not worth the time and effort, while peace and quiet takes no effort.

17.

We are free to roam this world at any time, but we are not free to roam our minds. Until we break through our own barriers to our higher thinking we will always be self-limiting.

18.

If we desire we will suffer, the best is close at hand when we think.

19.

When we find what is missing it will have been our higher thinking.

20.

The ability to govern our lives by our higher thinking will result in peacefulness.

21.

We all feel we know what gives us pleasure, but we have to think to know what gives us happiness. This is higher thinking functioning over feeling good.

22.

Standards of living are from our feelings, but quality of life is from our thinking.

23.

The burden of proof is the burden of life without thinking.

24.

Our higher thinking is like the dark side of the moon, we know it is there.

25.

Our thinking may just be the weakest link in our chain of events.

26.

We don't think when we desire and we don't desire when we think.

27.

We may feel our decisions are best for us, but feelings are not thinking until we think more and feel less for our lives to become meaningful.

28.
Wanting fills all our lives with desire for what is seemingly always missing. This unrest will never be fulfilled until we stop and think about our lives.

29.
We are our own advocate or adversary as determined by our motivations of feeling or thinking.

30.
All of our commitments have defined our limitations without knowing it.

31.
Aren't we deceived by our emotions to do what we wouldn't do if we thought about it?

32.
Maybe we don't know life because we haven't really been thinking; we've just been doing what feels good all our lives.

33.
We are weakened by our weaknesses and we are strengthened by our strengths; the obvious is somewhat difficult to comprehend if we don't think.

34.
Life's struggles are self-generated without us thinking.

35.
We live the life we felt about and not the life we thought about.

36.
We are but an appendage of our instincts when we're not thinking.

37.
When all we do is to feel good or bad then we're not thinking.

38.
We get a higher education so we can get a good job with more money for fun and excitement. This is always done without thinking.

39.
Emotions are motions away from a higher form of life.

40.
When we bore our senses, our higher thinking can be known, for in stillness is thoughtfulness.

41.
Do not act until you think about it; to be wise or to be foolish is a choice.

42.
We are imprisoned by our desires or freed by our thinking; one is a choice the other is not.

43.
All our battles in life were always with ourselves, but without knowing this we don't know our worst enemy is alive and well inside us.

44.
Owning a mansion is our emotional feeling, but owning a tent is our higher thinking.

45.
Our higher thinking is the hardest thing to do; we can know this by looking at the history of the human race and then ourselves.

46.
We are the problem of our suffering and discontent without knowing we can also be the solution by thinking more and feeling less.

47.
Fame or fortune is for pleasure, but peaceful and calm is for happiness. One is how we feel and the other is how we think.

48.
What is best for us and what is the most fun are never the same. Happiness is alone and pleasure is with others. One is our higher thinking and the other is our instinctive desires.

49.
Right or wrong shouldn't be determined by our feelings without thinking.

50.
We may be spiritual either from our higher thinking or our lower emotions, while one may be freeing the other was controlling.

51.
When our lives are discontented until we die something is just plain wrong with our feelings. We were actually not thinking but just feeling our way through life.

52.
If our highest thinking is just to be happy, then why is success always rewarded with pleasure?

53.
All our desires will result in stress and anxiety because we are feeling and not thinking.

54.
Life is so good when we think about it and not when we feel something is always missing in order to make life better.

55.
Those with higher thinking may go to new heights; the rest will have a lot more fun tonight.

56.
When choosing freely by one's own thinking, one must reject feelings.

57.
Our greatness is found in what we think instead of what we feel.

58.
We all know we want more, but when we know more we will want less.

59.
Life is so good when we think about it, but we feel we must always add something to make it better.

60.
We settle for what we feel; we should do what we think we should do.

61.
We will have pleasure by our instincts, but we will be happy by our higher thinking.

62.
We are self-limited by our desires or self-liberated by our thinking.

63.
Ours is a life of our making as we may feel and not by our thinking.

64.
We all feel that our life can be better, but we must think in order to make our life better.

65.
If we did what we thought, we wouldn't have done what we did.

66.
Our subjection to compulsion is all human bondage. Then our higher thinking is to resist the impulse to perform irrational acts.

67.
The chains that bind us are all self-inflicted; without thinking they will always exist.

68.
When we use our higher thinking over our instinctive desires and fears, all life has new motivation of meaningfulness, not just what feels good. This is most reliable not desirable.

69.

Our lives can be transformed by thinking or just the same desires. We made that decision long ago. Greatness is within our ability to imagine our future from our higher thinking and not our emotions.

70.

We may not see life clearly, but have become our own heaven or hell as the results of our thinking or feeling.

71.

Higher thinking doesn't desire pleasure or fear and pain.

72.

All of our lives we are doing what feels good and avoiding what doesn't without thinking about it.

73.

What we feel is not important, but what we think is.

74.

We may wear out our bodies while our minds hardly get used.

75.

This is either the best of times or the worst of times, as determined by our thinking or lack of thinking.

76.

Wisdom of the ages is our own higher thinking today.

77.

We are driven by our motivations or we are the driver by our highest thinking.

78.

Life is the purpose of life when we think, or it's for others or possessions when we feel.

79.

We may love our emotions, but that's the source of our stress and anxiety turmoil.

80.

Without us thinking we will never become aware of the cause of our actions.

81.

We aren't better because we don't think better; we do more for fear and pleasure. We're doing less thinking.

82.

We are the problem without our thinking in order to be the solution.

83.

When we have as much respect for all of life as we do for our own, higher thinking will come to the forefront as it should be.

84.

Our feeling of emotions are unbidden by our higher thinking.

85.

Fight or flee and desire or fear are emotions and not thinking.

86.

We do what we feel we must do and not what we think we must do.

87.

When we want it then we have to live with it, think about that first.

88.

The questions we never asked ourselves were the questions we never thought to ask.

89.

We will see life in the ways we want to feel, but think and then see life for real.

90.

The effects of the human race shows it is because we weren't thinking.

91.
Life is good when we think about it, but not so good when we feel something is missing all the time.

92.
We all know what desire and fear is from birth until death from our emotions and this is why it's so hard to think clearly in order to know what to do that's wisest for us.

93.
Our lives will get better by thinking or worse by feeling.

94.
Emotions are a liability, thinking is an asset.

95.
If we haven't got life figured out yet, it's because we haven't thought about it.

96.
A life without thinking is a life just doing what comes naturally.

97.
Life doesn't get any better when we think about it.

98.
When we don't think we won't know what to do, but just what feels good.

99.
We are prisoners of our emotions without thinking.

100.
When we don't think we don't know we're not thinking.

101.
We feel we know what to do, but when we think we really do know what to do.

102.
We don't think why we must do what we do except it just feels good. This is not reason or logic.

103.
Our life's experiences are the effects of our thinking or lack of thinking.

104.
We will either survive or thrive as determined by our thinking or feeling.

105.
Let our higher thinking govern our lower desires.

106.
Give ourselves a break from now and just be happy, but it's harder to think than it is to feel.

107.
Peace and quiet is boring to our senses, but happiness to our higher thinking.

108.
We're lost to our desires or we're found by our thinking.

109.
Some days I feel I'm too old to slay the dragon within, but then I start thinking again.

110.
We feel we know life or must think to know life.

111.
Our lives are frivolous without us thinking.

112.
We will fight or flee, one is feelings and the other is thinking.

113.
Life is so wonderful when we think about it.

114.
To respect our higher thinking over our lower desires is mind over body.

115.
Free time to do nothing is our highest thinking, without desire or fear that requires endless concern.

116.
We're always better than we feel we are, when we think about it.

117.
Without thinking we will cause harm to ourselves, yet our emotions rule our lives.

118.
We can only see as far as we can think, so we are the limitation of ourselves.

119.
We are coming apart at the seams, but we still feel we are doing it right. That's not really thinking all right.

120.
When we access our upper thinking there is no limit to our happiness.

121.
We are intentionally limited by our not thinking, wouldn't you say?

122.
An open mind is more we will know, but the less we think the less we know.

123.
Most of life doesn't think very much and most of the time we don't either.

124.
When we start to feel we've got life figured out our minds start to close to anything else.

125.
To the extent of our thinking will be the extent of our lives too.

126.
Our higher thinking is alone without fantasies.

127.
When we use our body a lot it just wears out, but when we use our minds a lot it just gets better.

128.
Our higher thinking is on a high shelf alone, out of the way of our daily decisions.

129.
When we write a lot we begin to know we don't know as much as we felt.

130.
Let us stop kidding ourselves; we do not think what we are doing.

131.
If we could think better, we would know better.

132.
We come to the level of our potential if we think and not feel.

133.
Life is good when we think about it.

134.
When we get tired of living, we haven't thought about life very well.

135.
When we want we are not free or happy.

136.
Life is so good, but we don't know it now. It's always yesterday or tomorrow that requires memory or speculation, so not real.

137.
If we don't know maybe we don't think.

138.
What a good life this becomes when we think about it.

139.
To think we are not thinking, is thinking.

140.
In the absence of our thinking lives desires not yet considered.

141.
We seem to have so much to discover because we have thought about it so little.

142.
Life becomes contented when we're connected to our higher thinking.

143.
We may feel we're going the right way when we are really going the wrong way without thinking.

144.
We are all undone by not thinking by our feelings. Why has nobody told us this?

145.
To become free from ourselves is to live by our upper thinking and not our lower feelings.

146.
Our mind goes where it wants to go when we don't think about it.

147.
We are not alone when we're in the presence of our higher thinking.

148.
Either up or down is determined by our thinking or feelings.

149.

We all do what we want, but that's not what we need, so stop, look, and listen. We could find a new way, but not the old way of not thinking.

150.

Loneliness may result in peace, quiet and calmness if we think about it.

151.

We must think about what we do not know, for what we do know is causing problems.

152.

Our life's rewards are quantity and not quality when we're not thinking clearly.

153.

We desire all that is missing in our lives, yet we don't desire clear thinking for peace and harmony. When we acquire clear thinking, we will know that nothing else is missing in our lives.

154.

We have to think that life is paradise before it becomes paradise in our lives too. We can find our way when we think first.

155.

Our gate to higher thinking is guarded from entry by our lower desires and fears.

156.

Instinct dictates all life, but with our higher thinking, we can as well.

157.

Everyone has made the decision between pleasure or happiness, which is from our instincts or from our thinking.

158.

To deviate from the tragedies of the human race, we only have to use our upper thinking.

159.
Life could be so easy, but we make it so hard because without thinking is not going to be the best way.

160.
We have developed a success orientated lifestyle of ambition instinctively for desire; we can only reverse this by our higher thinking.

161.
With our higher thinking there is no hurry or worry for we will all end the same.

162.
To breach our wall of emotions into our higher thinking is to find the peace, quiet, calm, tranquility, bliss and harmony we may never have found before.

163.
We are led by our emotions or we lead by our higher thinking. Emotions are our barrier.

164.
All things can interfere with our clear thinking.

165.
We are all held captive by unthinking or freed by thinking.

166.
There is a credibility gap between what we feel and what we think because feeling is not thinking. It's a different part of our minds and most unreliable.

167.
We must break through our ceiling into the attic of our mind, for there lives our highest thinking unknown to us.

168.
Our greatness must come from our highest thinking over our lowest desires and fears.

169.
Stress, anxiety, and despair overpower our influence of higher thinking.

170.
When we are less stressed, we are just thinking more clearly.

171.
We can't find our way very clearly when we are doing what we feel. We must think of our restrictions.

172.
If we never searched, we never found our calling, for our minds hold the depths or heights we may never have found.

173.
Progressive development is the knowledge from awareness of our inward state that restricts higher thinking.

174.
It is not what we feel between our thighs, but what we think behind our eyes that is important.

175.
The only way we will confront our confusion that brings us all to ruin is our higher thinking for unity of body and mind, and not just emotions.

176.
Imagination can manifest our future; we limit ourselves by not thinking.

177.
We are the alpha and omega of our thinking, for ourselves or not.

178.
The realization that life's causes are for our existence could be contrasted by our higher thinking.

179.
We are as free as our thinking and not our feeling.

180.
We are lost without our higher thinking; we must cope with our lower self's suffering.

181.
We're in a hurry to die when we're not thinking.

182.
We may learn more if we stopped to think.

183.
Our mind is more important because what entertains us is not thinking.

184.
Our inhibitions repress free thought.

185.
Death is the only deterrent to a wise person's pursuit of higher thinking.

186.
When we think we know is the same time we will stop learning.

187.
We are the results of our thinking, but of our not thinking even more.

188.
We are wrong when we think about it.

189.
We feel more without thinking.

190.
We feel all problems were meaningful, but feelings are meaningless if we're not thinking.

191.
Seeing comes before knowing may elude us.

192.
The time we think is the time well spent because the rest of our time has been wasted.

193.
Our thinking is outdated when we continue to do what did not work in the first place.

194.
Without thinking, an emptiness is within us.

195.
Wishful thinking: we all may wish for something, but that is not thinking.

196.
Our happiness is a fulfillment of an obligation our higher thinking has to ourselves.

197.
We are affected by the effects of our emotions or our thinking.

198.
We must do what we think and not what others feel is best for them.

199.
Pleasure and pain are ignorance, but wisdom is in the dualism of life. We won't know this if we are not thinking.

200.
This is the best or worst times of our lives, as determined by our motivation to feel good or to think good.

201.
Life is a race to the top or the bottom and those who have thought about it have a head start.

202.
Maybe what we don't know is only because we haven't thought about it. We may be very smart, but just have not thought about it.

203.

We go up or down, the choice is ours; we are only as good as we think we can become.

204.

The more we're outside the less we're inside and that's better for thinking clearly.

205.

Our mind can become in control of our senses, but we'll have to be older and surprise our senses.

206.

The absence of vanity and arrogance would allow us to surpass our limitations to a higher self.

207.

We are only as good as we think we are; how we think so we are.

208.

When we think wrong, we are wrong.

209.

All affairs of our heart are short circuits from our higher thinking mind.

210.

When all we strive for is fun and excitement there is going to be a lot of disappointment, sometimes more than we feel we can bear. This is not thinking.

211.

We are only as good as we think we can become.

212.

To identify our higher thinking, we must deny our desires or fears.

213.

So much to think about but so little time to think.

214.
We are expanded by our minds not our bodies.

215.
We can think better when we feel less.

216.
Our higher thinking realizes the cause and effects of life.

217.
Our life becomes a love or hate relationship without thinking about it.

218.
We are unhappy because we're not thinking but just feeling.

219.
We may feel our lives were thoughtful, but actually caused by not thinking.

220.
We are just as good as we feel we can be, or as great as we think we can be.

221.
Arose to my thinking at 3 am, mail is in as my pencil glides over paper, I'm now free from myself. Arise to your thinking or be as everyone else.

222.
We must catch on in order to let go, or we can let go in order to catch on. Our authority is with or without thinking.

223.
Are you thinking or are you feeling?

224.
We live by what we've got because we feel there isn't anymore. We haven't thought about life very much.

225.
I am alone without my thinking.

226.
So little time and so much to learn.

227.
If all we want is a good book then we're not thinking with our own mind.

228.
An open mind is an infinity of ideas without proof.

229.
We don't know we're not thinking when we feel we're thinking.

230.
When we always feel we're right, we will never think we're wrong because feelings aren't thinking.

231.
When we fear ourselves we know we are the unknown.

232.
We may feel that we think for ourselves, but nobody is thinking when feeling.

233.
We can't think clearly in the daytime because there is so much to see we must in turn do.

234.
We feel happiness is boring without thinking.

235.
We are maybe better at drinking than we are at thinking, but we must know that.

236.
Life becomes more meaningful when we think about it.

237.
Losers blame others so they feel confident. Winners blame themselves so they can become confident.

238.
The more you think about thinking is to become thoughtful of life and ourselves.

239.
We must think to know we're unhappy.

240.
When we feel we're down we must think to be up.

241.
We are only as good as we think we are.

242.
The harder we work the less we think.

243.
We will feel until we die or we will think to live.

244.
Desire will interfere with our thinking without thinking.

245.
We must still our desires so our thinking can come through.

246.
For our loves we would do anything but think.

247.
Life's harder when we don't think.

248.
We possess higher thinking without the desire of its use.

249.
That we have two minds is unknown to almost everybody.

250.
Meet me half way to know a better way.

251.
Our higher thinking is available in our lives for happiness, but we only desire pleasure.

252.
We go up into our higher thinking or down into our desires and fears.

253.
Emotions will strengthen our bodies, but thinking will strengthen our minds.

254.
When our higher thinking is better than our emotional decisions, our lives will be wiser.

255.
We will progress to a point of competence by the degree of our thinking.

256.
If you think about it, slavery is a choice.

257.
This could be the best times of our lives if we think about it.

258.
We've desired the chains that bind us without thinking clearly.

259.
We must think to be free of the bondage of emotions.

260.
We stand in our way when it's a way without thinking.

261.
We are enslaved by desires and freed by thinking.

262.
Societies advance to a point of incompetence, but our higher thinking can advance to a point of competence.

263.
Our emotions are natural to survive but our higher thinking is unnatural to thrive.

264.
To think we are in heaven will make us happier than to feel we are in hell.

265.
To either survive or to thrive is a choice if we think about it.

266.
Our higher thinking can be found between the flattened spaces on each side of the forehead.

267.
Know our higher thinking as the whole self and not our emotional biases.

268.
We are blown to and from by the winds of desire. We are stilled and calmed by our higher thinking.

269.
We must control ourselves or we are in turn controlled by others.

270.
To test, check and verify by evidence or experiment is our self-control.

271.
Our well-being may have more value than we placed on it.

272.
We hate those who hate us and we like those who like us, you would think everyone would know that.

273.
Our lives will unfold by our choices, yet we are unhappy by our choices. That should give cause for introspection.

274.
In the stillness of our higher thinking dwells consciousness, empathy, wisdom, enlightenment.

275.
Cause no harm and take no possessions or we will surely suffer the consequences.

276.
Our senses will tell us what to do but our higher thinking will tell us what not to do.

277.
Work maybe without thinking and thinking maybe without work.

278.
Our higher thinking is elusive and intangible but necessary for the creation of happiness that is elusive and intangible.

279.
What we know and love is very evident but our higher thinking is barely known by anyone.

280.
The higher thinking knows life without effort that others may reject as troublesome.

281.
We are transfixed by our emotions but transformed by our higher thinking.

282.
We are empowered when we become what we think.

283.
What is real and what is a fantasy must be determined by our higher thinking and not our emotions.

284.
We will become the best or worst boss of ourselves as determined by our thinking.

285.
If we don't want to live with it then don't do it.

286.
Our minds are either a tool for us to become happy or a weapon against us for pleasure.

CHAPTER TWELVE

WISDOM:
To produce a given event

1.
Wisdom is a prediction that for an exhaustive set of outcomes we can produce a given event from the total number of possible outcomes. This is accomplished prior to any action.

2.
Intelligence is the quantity of thinking but wisdom is the quality of thinking.

3.
Our higher intellect will not give us free will over our heredity and environment because that would take our wisdom.

4.
When we are prepared for anything that life may give then we are wise.

5.
Our failure of wisdom and understanding results is a long arduous life with severe disappointment.

6.
The mind will kill the body from desires and fears, or the body will kill the mind from old age and wisdom.

7.
Our power of imaginative thinking is inconceivably good. That's the human minds capability of apprehending reality over appearance.

8.
A fool feels better, but a wise person knows better.

9.

The greatest good is the knowledge of the union our mind has with itself.

10.

We all work for money: wouldn't we be better off if we worked for wisdom instead?

11.

We need to know timing to stay or go, when to quit, for a wise person must know all three.

12.

The means doesn't justify the end because it's the journey that is meaningful or not.

13.

We want to feel good all our lives without ever having to think about it, that's how our emotions work by a lack of good judgement or common sense.

14.

We must catch on in order to let go or we will always be the same as we are now. When we don't see our limitations we can't see what to change and will always be living at our limitations.

15.

We can only stop the rat race when we realize it was always in our head.

16.

Greatness is in the wisdom we acquired and not in the pleasure we desired.

17.

Our insights into ourselves will affect our lives in a positive way. Without this rudder of wisdom we are adrift to the winds of fate.

18.

Information and knowledge is essential for the wisdom to understand life and ourselves as the basis to act.

19.

Wisdom is a persistent preoccupation with reasonable ideas.

20.

Wisdom of the ages was acquired without books, desires or fear, but from being alone in nature, using our higher thinking.

21.

We can always have pleasure, but we can't let pleasure have us to the extent we could never be happy. To that degree is our wisdom.

22.

Our successful apprehension of facts and propositions and their relationships to reality will either result in a life of wealth or contentment.

23.

Wisdom is the objective of an extended difficult quest. That was no trouble at all.

24.

To finally know life and ourselves is not easy, but to try to explain to others who don't even want to know is even harder. The greatest value of our wisdom is helping us, not others.

25.

We are all basic: it required wisdom to become complex in order to live simply.

26.

Wisdom is without pleasure and pleasure is without wisdom.

27.

That we are the cause of life's problems makes a solution very difficult to comprehend.

28.

Without doubt there is failure and without failure there is no doubt.

29.

We go anywhere we want and do anything we like with knowledge, power and will, when we are wise.

30.

Wisdom is doing what is needed to be done to be happy and not what we wanted to do to have pleasure.

31.

We don't know we are dysfunctional is the reason why we are dysfunctional.

32.

To see life clearly and direct us to a higher form of life is the hardest thing to do. This is evident because so few can make themselves do what's best.

33.

Faith is a desire for pleasure and fear of pain, but not reason or logic. While knowing ignorance is wisdom, ignoring wisdom is foolish.

34.

In the silence of our minds, rests the wisdom of the ages.

35.

If life seems too good to be true, that is when we should know we are wise.

36.

We have mental assets and mental liabilities: a wise person knows them one and all but knows better than to play with fire.

37.

It is really not what we have that's important, it's what we don't want to have that saves all our time for ourselves.

38.

If we wake up wise tomorrow we would do nothing we did today.

39.

Our greatness is in the ability to govern ourselves wisely.

40.
Of all the people we have ever known, we may have never known a wise person.

41.
The most disturbing aspect in our lives is when we think about that it was always us. We are always the last one to realize this after we've tried everything else.

42.
A wise person knows the difference between pleasure and happiness is ourselves.

43.
When we let our wisdom be our guide, we are happy without pleasure.

44.
When controlling ourselves we are controlling what controls us.

45.
To have known but a few wise people is better than to have known many others. All can be counted on one hand and have fingers unused.

46.
Submission or obsession? Less or more? While less is clearer, more is confusing. A wise person thinks he knows the way, but a fool feels he does too.

47.
The more we have the more we want, and the less we have the less we want. Who is wise and who is not?

48.
We will come out of our self-made prison to freedom just by controlling ourselves.

49.
A wise person never experiences difficulties because they don't confront them, and knows we are defeated by ourselves.

50.
The greatest weakness we can overcome is our greatest accomplishment because that's how far we have come.

51.
We are conditioned from birth by wrong thinking that takes a lifetime to correct.

52.
We seem to be in a hurry to die otherwise we would be trying to notice life's details along the way.

53.
To possess total recall is not as significant as the application of wisdom.

54.
Without a doubt we'll stay where we are now. For doubts are our checks and balances.

55.
All life is controlled by its instinctual desires and fears, but only the human race can know this and be the control of its causes.

56.
There is the power of the pen but our wisdom is in the power of the eraser to make life meaningful.

57.
When we are wise, it's our time to drive and not to be driven.

58.
We limit our lives by our feelings. When we know this to be true we many never trust our feelings. Surely wisdom must be close at hand now.

59.
Let's be firm, let's be wise.

60.
Wisdom is to know what to do at any given time in our life is timing. What time is it now?

61.
We should admire wisdom over anything else, but it is not fun or even exciting.

62.
Let our minds be closed by intelligence and wisdom, but not ignorance and bigotry.

63.
Our lives are the results of us seeking either pleasure or happiness, so be wise.

64.
Wisdom must be sought to be in our lives.

65.
All hardships will make us stronger or weaker as to be determined by more or less wisdom.

66.
Wisdom serves us best because no one else wants to listen.

67.
Our wisdom comes from within us because no one else seems to be able to tell us.

68.
The hardest thing is to define the problem in our lives. When it is us, we don't know or we wouldn't have any problem in the first place.

69.
By seeing our voids, we have confirmed our suspicions.

70.
It is going to be lonely when we are trying to be wise.

71.

All wisdom is to have knowledge, influence and will over ourselves by avoiding the downfalls of everyone else.

72.

A wise mind knows what to do at any given time. All our lives we are known by the mistakes we make.

73.

Ignorance and fools rule others, but a wise person rules themselves.

74.

Wisdom must have to be a pathway alone, for the power of others over us is for the pleasure we must give in return.

75.

Wisdom is our understanding of the enemy within us that others are unaware of.

76.

To go where no one desires to go is into the wisdom of our minds, because it's not fun or exciting.

77.

What's most significant is the wisdom we possess.

78.

To undergo difficulties gives us the ability to withstand adversity so as to continue unyielding in our convictions.

79.

Wisdom is in not having to make the trip at all.

80.

We must become wise in order to recognize wisdom.

81.

We would have to give all that we have to have wisdom.

82.
The right choices are easy but the wrong choices are hard because life is easy for the wise.

83.
When we would rather be happy than to have pleasure we will have learned the wisdom of the ages.

84.
If wisdom only knows the differences between pleasure and happiness then that is all it needs to know.

85.
Pleasure is with friends and family while happiness is alone in nature: those who know this are wise.

86.
Life is the purpose of life; to the degree that we know this we are wise.

87.
Our value is to be determined by pleasure or happiness, this is our two minds whole life's struggle.

88.
Knowledge is not understanding, therefore intelligence is not wisdom.

89.
Our brains could become the biggest organ in our bodies.

90.
By limiting the amount of money we desire to feel secure, we are also limiting our ego's lust and fear.

91.
A conversation with ourselves is a meeting of our cerebral cortex and our emotions. That's either for happiness or pleasure.

92.
The best way is not the fastest way because time should not be seen as a shortcut, but a life.

93.
The greatest meaning in life is for those who can discriminate quality of life and not standard living.

94.
We think we're smart because we know what we want, but we're not because we don't know why we want what we want.

95.
We may choose either to become rich physically or rich mentally.

96.
When we think nothing good will come out of life, the secret is just knowing what is feeling and what is thinking. When something feels good, look out.

97.
If we are intelligent that's a false sense of wisdom.

98.
Wisdom is not knowing when to fold or when to raise, but not to play.

99.
We are always right when we watch out not to be wrong.

100.
It doesn't make much sense to travel to far off countries to find other people, when we haven't even found ourselves.

101.
The only thing we have in life is ourselves, because possessions or others may come and go, so be kind to ourselves.

102.
Power over us is a lack of influence over others.

103.
What comes first, wisdom or solitude? We must have wisdom to have solitude or we must have solitude to have wisdom. That's the wisdom of the ages.

104.
Our higher system of thought advocates a natural belief based on human reasoning of the laws of the universe.

105.
Avoid the negative and accentuate the positive is child and dog psychology, yet not good enough advice for all of us.

106.
In life it is not the package but the contents that determine our fate.

107.
All of the turmoil in life is just our inability to see life and ourselves clearly.

108.
To always find fault in others is to never know oneself.

109.
All of life is not as it seems to be, but as it is.

110.
We all know meaningless well because we are doing it all our lives without knowing it.

111.
It is good to age when we are wise because we will get what we deserve.

112.
We can read all the books we want, but that will not give us good judgement.

113.
When we overcome ourselves we are then gentle and accepting.

114.

Since we cannot touch our mind the next best thing is to be in touch with our mind.

115.

The obvious is in the way of any discovery. We look for what we want to see and not for what's real.

116.

We are all hiding from what's inside of us, otherwise we might know why we do what we must.

117.

We are all controlled by our desires, prestige, money, possessions, jobs, family, friends, homes, lust, fear, hunger, loneliness, sickness, and death. We are not controlled by logic and reason.

118.

By simplifying our lives there is less that needs to be done and more time to be living.

119.

The gauge of our success should be measured in the distance traveled mentally form birth till death.

120.

What we feel is meaningful is meaningless, but what we think is meaningless is meaningful.

121.

A wise person will never have made problems for themselves, but time and change will play havoc with us all.

122.

We have to learn to postpone gratification in order to realize an ability to find what's actually missing within us.

123.

Monkey sees; monkey does. Wise person sees; a wise person does not do.

124.
We'll have an eternity of nothingness so how important is now? Our lives are everything, so very humbling, too.

125.
Life will never get any better than we can comprehend, so we may be the weakest link.

126.
Intelligence coupled with wisdom is like a kite with a tail.

127.
Mindfulness should come before actfulness, but it does not.

128.
When we think about it, our end is forever, so think about how important now really is to be alive.

129.
Our ends can't justify our daily lives.

130.
We must choose either wealth or wisdom because we can only have one.

131.
Life has baggage, but only if we pick it up.

132.
All life is in transition and wisdom is in anticipation.

133.
Wisdom stands the test of time.

134.
Now are the best times of our lives, except we don't know it.

135.
Life should not be measured in the quantity of years we live, but in the quality of life we experienced.

136.
The only value of wisdom is to be found in its usage.

137.
We may have known many people in our life, but never known a wise person so would not know what wisdom does.

138.
When we exchange one self-made prison for another, our life becomes the burden of proof.

139.
We go where we feel, but every new day is a habitual limitation of not thinking. Then surely we would know this if we were really wise.

140.
There is an unknown reality of our mind's inability to be governed by reason or logic.

141.
We can't convince anyone of their ignorance for they find fault with others, but a wise person is quick to blame themselves.

142.
We all have goals, but to have meaningful goals we must be wise.

143.
Our choices will reinforce or diminish all life's experiences.

144.
A closed mind works just like no mind.

145.
The best way is not the fun way.

146.
Enslaved by our feelings or freed by our reasoning?

147.
Our mind is a wonderful thing when we don't ignore it by rationalizations.

148.
We will know as much as our decision to reason.

149.
Life shouldn't be measured by the quantity of pleasures, but by the quality of experiences from our mental acuity.

150.
Simplicity is good, and wisdom is good.

151.
Life's demands on us are precluded by the exclusion of any reason or logic.

152.
The futility of life's trifles is a fruitless abyss.

153.
As we are, we just have more baggage unless we figure our life out: those superficial and intrusive things we could bring under our own command and control.

154.
We distinguish our mind's ability to know itself for our own good.

155.
Wisdom is served by increased happiness.

156.
All good, bad or indifference is confidence to risk, but ego, lust, and fear is our bondage.

157.
The strongest passions we can refrain from are our greatest accomplishments.

158.
Supreme guidance, provider and protector of our life are the power of discernment.

159.

We should learn acceptance and understanding of life on its terms and not our own pre-conceived opinion on how it suits us best.

160.

We are the best or worst in life simply due to our thinking or not thinking. Our wisdom is in knowing the difference.

161.

To want less is to have more, for those who want less will know this is true.

162.

We are all at our best when we know timing.

163.

The person who dies with the least possessions is the true winner.

164.

We are living outside of our thinking. Otherwise our lives would be thoughtful.

165.

The answer to life's demands lies within our mind's ability to know ourselves and our life clearly.

166.

Our human struggle is always between emotions: that's the lack of reason or logic. We're controlled by our weaknesses and not our strengths.

167.

Pleasure isn't fulfilling because it requires repetitiveness, but discipline to control ourselves is for our greater good.

168.

A wise person teaches change, but all beliefs are imprisoning.

169.

When we have wisdom we are foolish if we don't use it.

170.
The wisest results are those that are determined by our reasoning, for the best results are without excuses.

171.
We seem to wear ourselves out when we're going the wrong way.

172.
The more we add to our lives the more we are subtracting from it, except life's wisdom that we accepted.

173.
Are we driven by life's causes or driven by our wisdom?

174.
Our wisdom just saves us from ourselves.

175.
We don't appreciate anything as much as when we are just getting ready to lose it because of wisdom.

176.
Some need to be told what to do, but its best to know what not to do.

177.
We are not killing time, for it's time that is killing us.

178.
We need to be self-directed not self-inflicted.

179.
Wisdom gives us insight.

180.
Wisdom is not easy or everyone would be wise. For the finer things in life are also the rarest.

181.
All possessions are prisons of ego, lust and fear.

182.
We only have what we settled for.

183.
We are the wisest person around when we take time out for this moment.

184.
We will not notice what we are not looking for.

185.
Everyone progresses as far as they can or cannot, but the essence of our life is our choices.

186.
We are either the storm in our life or the calm in the storm of life. All the wisdom in life can become ours by the way of our thinking.

187.
Wisdom is knowing not to pursue desires or fears.

188.
We are the source of our limitation and without knowing will always be.

189.
To have influence over ourselves, we must test, check and verify the evidence with experience.

190.
Creativity is adaption to change.

191.
When we question our motives we will learn about ourselves.

192.
Mistakes are an opportunity for change, success, knowledge, insight, thought, resolve, and adaption, but without will there is no way.

193.
Appreciation is the result of our wisdom.

194.
Wise people must be hard to find because there are so few.

195.
Our lives are a labor of pleasure or a labor of happiness by the amounts of wisdom we can bring to bear.

196.
What we don't know is not bothering us enough yet, or we would be searching for wisdom now.

197.
Wisdom is to know we are the source of our own life's experiences and to predetermine beforehand the results of our life over our instincts.

198.
Wisdom is from knowledge, influence and will.

199.
Know if we are opinionated on everything then we may never learn anything.

200.
When we don't know we will do just as we are doing.

201.
One wise person is worth more than a world of fools, but doesn't acknowledge themselves.

202.
When we feel wronged we in turn do the same back. This is a self-destructive race to the bottom so nobody wins except ignorance of our emotions.

203.
We're going to become history very soon, so make our lives good or bad now.

204.
Wisdom is in knowing how to become happy.

205.
We are better off by doing the opposite of what we feel we should do.

206.
Low life is a close neighbor to high life. We can go there any time we want.

207.
We limit our wisdom without knowing, by restricting our knowing.

208.
Maybe if we knew we were running too hard we would be wise; all that we know may not be us.

209.
Living a deliberate life is what we want to do and not what we have to do.

210.
When we are wise we are ruled by our higher thinking and none other.

211.
Mind over body is the result of our influence. Through acceptance is our fruit of cultivating ourselves.

212.
We are unhappy because we are unwise.

213.
We will go where our minds go, either as we feel or think. When we know this we could become wise.

214.
We must control ourselves or we will be controlled by others.

215.
Life becomes much simpler when we know what not to do.

216.
Wisdom may come as the result of our individual reasoning, but not our desires. Then to the degree of our thoughts we will be wise.

217.
We are limited or liberated by ourselves.

218.
Our greatest experiences are the effects of our mind's ability to know itself and then direct itself.

219.
Self-inflicted conflict isn't evident and this refusal to acknowledge will always cause us suffering.

220.
We wouldn't know a wise person if we're not looking, or no one told us.

221.
Our means to govern ourselves is not the best because we have the mind of a child.

222.
We all know what we want to do, but few know what they should do.

223.
All peace or war is the dualism within us.

224.
It helps to write to know ourselves better.

225.
We can only see what we are looking for and, in this way we will get what we seek.

226.
Life is much more when it becomes a meaningful and not a meaningless experience.

227.
We cannot make a commitment or we will become a prisoner unto ourselves.

228.
Since all good things must come to an end, we should not seek things.

229.
To see ourselves clearly we have to become present in actually what are we doing now in our lives.

230.
Why would anyone do what hurts? Think on this and be wise.

231.
Our decisions should not be made by what we can do, but instead we should make up our minds what's best for us to do.

232.
When we don't go ahead then we stay behind.

233.
When we can say we did not think we could be this happy then we are wiser than we thought we could be.

234.
If we can't stop what's in us, it had better be right, for if we are wrong we will suffer.

235.
We can't move forward until we know where we are at now.

236.
Wisdom, prudence and good judgement is acquired through experience and reflection.

237.
We must beat a small path to our higher thinking so as to become a freeway to wisdom.

238.
Wisdom is always the most elusive, but also the greatest happiness.

239.
If we were wise we would be happy already.

240.
The maximum effect with the least effort is knowing timing.

241.
We seem to be driven all over the place when we are not the drivers.

242.
Wisdom is in knowing we don't need others to be happy.

243.
It is a waste of time dwelling on the memories of our past or the fear of the future because it is affecting us now, that is all that really matters.

244.
We can't let go so that's why we are let down. Even when we know this we still can't let go.

245.
Do we want to have pleasure or be in charge of ourselves? While one will suffer the other is free.

246.
We are controlled by what controls us. Think on this and be wise.

247.
Are we in control of our lives or are our lives in control of us?

248.
It would take knowledge, influence and will to take charge of ourselves.

249.

To purge the urge to have it all with our desires subdued, enabled us to see clearly.

250.

Our body owns the mind or the mind owns the body. Think on this and be wise.

251.

Adversity is opposed to one's interests, resulting in tensions or extensions. The axis of growth is our influence to act by intellect not emotions to or from a higher form of life.

252.

Our lives are not apparent from our senses or intellect, but are a result of intuition, insight and experience for an ultimate reality.

253.

We are confined by our possessions or we are liberated without possessions.

254.

Life is diminished yet replenished by its death.

255.

Life is the best game around when we learn how to play it.

256.

The greatest accomplishments are those that the fewest know. Finer things in life are the rarest to find: peace, calm, tranquility, blissfulness and harmony.

257.

We may see great distances when we stop to look.

258.

Let our mistakes be made in our thinking by not acting upon them.

259.

We are complacent because of our dysfunction to see ourselves clearly.

260.
We all know what's meaningless, but very few know what's meaningful.

261.
What we hold onto the tightest seems to hold us the most.

262.
Our instinctual emotions have us in total submission without our knowledge, power or influence.

263.
We may be at the top of the food chain, but we have yet to tame ourselves.

264.
To be in the know is to be in the hunt, no will no way.

265.
We are where our minds are right now.

266.
Life is the finest when we are the boss of ourselves.

267.
Through our personal experiences we acquire knowledge that in turn, with discipline, can be applied to our lives so as to cause a meaningful tomorrow.

268.
Our greatness comes from our minds and isn't a burden on us.

269.
When we hurry, we will gain or when we slow down, we will gain. This is a moment in our two mind's way of feeling or thinking.

270.
We could control what is controlling us: ego, lust and fear, which is money, sex and time. That is meaningless.

271.

We must cope with ourselves by becoming our own project or always struggling to be what we are not.

272.

Either time runs us or we run time. That's to be controlled by our weaknesses or controlled by our strengths.

273.

We are controlled by our feelings or we control by our minds.

274.

To acquire a meaningful life we must know what a meaningless life we have.

275.

When we look up and not down we can get it right because it's a race to the top or a race to the bottom, our choice.

276.

It is a lot later than we ever want to think.

277.

Our mind's total capacity is only limited by our emotions.

278.

Up and up into our higher thinking, or down and down into our despair, the choice was not ours without us knowing.

279.

The ghosts of our past affect the realities of the present to alter our futures.

280.

We settle for less when we could have so much more.

281.

We may receive the life that we can perceive.

282.

We are the effects of our thinking or feelings.

283.
Wisdom is like medicine, we may know we could get better if we take it, but do not.

284.
Wisdom is calmness of our emotions for judgement.

285.
Look at you: you don't look anything like yourself. When we look into the mirror that's a credibility gap in how we see life and how we see ourselves.

286.
We must evolve in our lives to become happier and well-adjusted by taking ownership of our thinking and desires.

287.
We're driven by our senses or we're driven by our common sense.

288.
When we mate for minds and not for looks this world and our lives will be a much better place. That is to look better or think better; this is the choice we all must make.

289.
Life is backwards because as we get closer to the end we are just starting to figure life out.

290.
When we finally know what is meaningful, our life as we knew it was meaningless.

291.
Our curiosity is ideas for discovery by exploring our mind, we must write for self-discovery.

292.
Reasons are our reasoning with ourselves.

293.
When we control what controls us, we simply have control over ourselves.

294.
We must save us from ourselves so we can be safe and happy as long as possible.

295.
The more we want the less we think, for wants are endless, but needs are right now.

296.
We already know our past and present so we must change to make our future even better.

297.
We must trust in our wisdom or always fear life.

298.
When we know how to take charge of ourselves we will change.

299.
What is the best for us, desire or reason? See this as a learning moment of will.

300.
We will always get older, but we may not get wiser if we don't think about it at all.

301.
What we feel was meaningful was actually meaningless. If we think about it we would be better off to just keep our life simple.

302.
We may wonder why we can't be happy; it's because we have never thought about it.

303.
Death is the price we must pay for living.

304.
Without self-restricting our feelings, we are without influence over ourselves.

305.
Life is not just to do, but to be.

306.
When the removal of desires tensions is done by reason we eliminated time, money and effort also stress, anxiety and despair.

307.
To do is externally independent of our mind but to be is to remain independent, undisturbed and uninterrupted.

308.
All true success is just in knowing what to pursue.

309.
Take risk only when you are wise, otherwise stay home.

310.
Mining our minds is searching for the causes of wisdom and the timing of our time.

311.
Our lives are spent in hunting or nesting. Wisdom is to know what's meaningful because we can't take the nest with us.

312.
Rise to a decisive point above us; otherwise we will have to live with ourselves.

313.
Our lives are like the sands in an hourglass of life; to be lived as we pass through a focal point to rest eternally with all the other grains of sand.

314.
Emotions or thinking are a choice.

315.
Wisdom stands the test of time.

316.
Discontent is just an opportunity, for the unattachment or attachment is the effects of desires.

317.
We can run or we can hide, but we can't run and hide. This is how our two minds work; one is driven while the other is the driver. We will not see this if we don't look.

318.
We are all suffering, but some less than others because they know it.

319.
Maybe if we knew better we would do better.

320.
Submitting to authority and controlling ourselves is not easy.

321.
Our minds can become our strengths and not just our weaknesses.

322.
When we find what we were seeking, then the seeking will end.

323.
Our life expectancy is what we expect from life instead of from ourselves.

324.
We progress to a point of incompetence, for wisdom is determined by our higher thinking and not by our desires or fears.

325.
Our mind can be a leveling force in a life of opposing forces.

326.
Our wisdom is not to work so as to have pleasure.

327.
The source of our strength cannot be the source of our weaknesses too.

328.
How can we be wise if we don't know what wisdom is?

329.
An entity can pass into fulfillment by its opposites through the means of parallel ideas.

330.
Our essence is real, but faith is an illusion and intangible. That's the difference between darkness and the light. While one may feel better, it is still darkness.

331.
Be wise or be unhappy, our choice.

332.
We have to realize we are the problem before we can become our solution.

333.
We are without a doubt most complex to figure out.

334.
We have to know what not to do before we may know what to do.

335.
The difference between emotions and thinking is wisdom.

336.
Why would anyone strive for fame or fortune when we can see what it does to anyone who tries or succeeds.

337.
Wisdom is always denied by fools.

338.
Our essence is the cause of our life's experiences.

339.
Aren't our minds either an asset or liability, as determined by our choices?

340.
We are controlled or we control ourselves.

341.
Comfort only comes from deep within us and not our egos, lust and fear.

342.
We are alive so we must think of what life is to us. Where we came from we shall also go.

343.
Now is our time of our life, but how much more important this knowledge is when it is realized.

344.
We are driven by our thoughts of life, unless we consider being our own thinker.

345.
Wisdom over emotions is mind over matter.

346.
Our mind is the camp of our enemy. We didn't even know this.

347.
We may never know our strengths because of our weaknesses.

348.
A life career was our choice.

349.
We seem to be always in a hurry to die until we get close to the end, and then we want to slow down a little bit.

350.
We should mate at an older age so as to pass on some wisdom. When we mate so young, we just pass on our instincts.

351.
Life doesn't get any better except for us knowing it.

352.
We can learn to respect ourselves more than we do.

353.
Come up with a plan or go down with the ship.

354.
Opportunists have shed the old to have the new.

355.
We are driven by life's demands on us, or we are our driver of the rewards of living.

356.
When life pushes we must pull and when life pulls we must push.

357.
We must come up to the challenges of life or we will be left in the dust of the ages.

358.
When we don't know we are the problem then we can't become the solution.

359.
We are limited by our limitations.

360.
Our minds torment us or can free us from ourselves.

361.
All of our life's struggles will have been our choice.

362.
Location, location, location, but we don't listen.

363.
The body controls the mind, but the mind can learn to control the body.

364.
Life is not savored when multi-tasking.

365.
Wisdom is liberating.

366.
Life is too precious to give to anyone else.

367.
We know not what we need and we need not what we want.

368.
All that we own shows our limitations.

369.
People are far more interesting than their function or experiences.

370.
Our best effort will become the contentment of our life.

371.
We like those who like us and when we dislike others they will dislike us. This is why we become our own destiny of likes and dislikes.

372.
Life is our time to seek experiences for great insights.

373.
Cognitive insights will come from receptiveness to introspection.

374.
When a trophy life needs a trophy mate we are life's trophy and life is not our trophy.

375.
We own our lives or our lives own us.

376.
When to let go and when to hold will determine who we are now.

377.
Our lives become better or worse due to our essence.

378.
Our greatest good is the union of our minds without the desires or emotions.

379.
Introspection is a source for our future changes.

380.
Our life is limited by the hardships we chose without thinking.

381.
We control our lives or our lives control us.

382.
Life's greatest good is always quality and not quantity.

383.
We must exceed our expectations in order to live up to our capacity to eliminate our credibility gap.

384.
We run our life or our life runs us.

385.
We could be better than we are if we thought about ourselves and not about others.

386.
Let the wisdom of the ages meet our ability to understand ourselves for meaningful goals.

387.
Death completes life.

388.
We must seek the wisdom of the ages because these are confusing times.

389.
We feel our life is lacking and something needs to be done to fix it. Life is not broken and we don't have to change it to suit us.

390.
We may read for inspiration, but we must become our own inspiration.

391.
We must lack knowledge, influence, and will in order to be better than our current actions are now.

392.
A wise person runs from their weaknesses, but a fool runs toward their weaknesses and knows it.

393.
To do or not to do, therein lies our wisdom.

394.
We cannot have wealth and wisdom because wealth is for pleasure and wisdom is for happiness.

395.
Wisdom is very rare and difficult. That's why so few have wisdom, but most things rare are also most prized.

396.
What good is wisdom to a fool?

397.
Wisdom precedes our awareness of it.

398.
We get our education from others, but we get our wisdom from ourselves.

399.
Wisdom is in plain sight, but we don't desire to know because it's not fun or exciting.

400.
Do you want to feel good? Or do you want to be good?

401.
Wisdom is to seek a deliberate life above all else.

402.
We must will our thinking and in this way we will become wise.

403.
There is a wise way in our life, but we must say no to foolishness.

404.
Quit when desire is not sustainable.

405.
I've been young and foolish and old and wise; what a great improvement on my life.

406.
Life is best known without the trauma we bestow on it.

407.
Our wisdom is in just knowing what not to do and when not to do it.

408.
To possess will without wisdom is as bad as wisdom without will.

409.
Wisdom is like enlightenment in the fact it's not fun or exciting, so few are going to look there.

410.
The path of least resistance is a freeway to the wise person.

411.
All life is ruled by instinct or emotions. When we know this we could rule ourselves.

412.
Follow our desires or follow our wisdom is our life today.

413.
Wisdom is in the pathway we travel and not in the pathway we aspired to travel.

414.
It is desire that knows what to do but it's wisdom that knows what not to do.

415.
The wise person knows not to acquire what needs to be stored up so as to live free.

416.
We are much wiser to trade anger for kindness than anger for anger; then we won't have any enemies.

417.
Disagreements result in disaster but agreements results in masters of our fate.

418.
A wise person needs very little because possessions are no longer required anymore.

419.
Wisdom is much easier to understand than it is to follow.

420.
To be unknown, not honored and misunderstood is to be self-sufficient, independent and wise.

421.
Our lives are to have wisdom for what's best and reject all the rest.

422.
Restraint is our wisdom that lives inside the eyes of the beholder.

423.
The beginning of our wisdom is a wonder filled life.

424.
When our grip is firm on the wisdom of life and not on the facts of life our energy is not wasted running about any longer.

425.
The wise have a mind of their own but the foolish have the minds of others.

426.
The wise are peaceful and quiet but others see them as confused and misguided.

427.
We will be known either as leaders or followers, but the unknown are the wisest of them all.

428.
Wisdom knows what to do without doing, what works without working, and what fails without failing.

429.
In the pursuit of possessions, something is acquired every day, but in the pursuit of wisdom something is discarded every day.

430.
We can learn wisdom from the unwise because they're so plentiful.

431.
We are well aware of the emotions of actions while unaware of the wisdom of yielding.

432.
When we are unsure of our goals anymore this is actually us approaching the gates of wisdom.

433.
We are well aware of what's missing in our lives except our wisdom or happiness.

434.
Who knows when to stop and who knows when to go? Only wisdom does.

435.
We have our power in two ways: either over others or over ourselves.

436.
Money seems not to know when is enough. Wisdom knows not to chase fantasies.

437.
The wise avoid the extremes by knowing the limits and avoids changing others in order to change themselves.

438.
We must use the tools that will help us and avoid the tools that will harm us, for any harm to others will harm us too.

439.
To be restless is unattached, to be loose is without roots, to be masters of ourselves we must know this to be true.

440.
When we have experienced financial success we must be aware of all the harm that will cause us.

441.
When we rebuff all wisdom we can then have wealth, possessions, houses, families and friends.

442.
It is better to quit sooner than later for in all success lays our failure.

443.
When we become at peace we are freed from within, for through submission are the gates of wisdom.

444.
Always chasing after possessions is a madding life because we are going the wrong way; for wisdom chooses what is good and not what feels good.

445.
When gain or loss becomes unimportant we can trust in our life's new course.

446.
We know the desire of our senses naturally but they're indefinable by reason or logic.

447.
Our choice of attachments or detachments may be the most significant decision in our life.

448.
Our life maybe exhausting because we let it be so, or life is exuberating because we let it be so.

449.
The sensual seek gratification of their body and the wise seek gratification of their minds.

450.
Open-minded is one who opens untraveled regions of their minds in order to find a better life.

451.
Pleasures are no substitute for happiness, like feelings are no substitute for thinking.

452.
The baggage we carry is a hardship we may not acknowledge, but a wise person vows not to pick up the baggage anymore.

453.
Frugality is satisfaction in not having to carry any baggage any more.

454.
When we realize our mind knows experiences can have great value in order to become a wiser person.

455.
Through wisdom we can meet all of life's challenges with the confidence and resolve from all life's experiences.

456.
When our goals are meaningful we will not be disillusioned.

CHAPTER THIRTEEN

PEACE:
Just peace from ourselves

1.
To give up our whole life's endeavors for just one thing would be worthwhile if that one thing was just peace from ourselves.

2.
The price we pay for our peace of mind is all our desires and fears.

3.
The most peaceful place can only be peaceful if we are too.

4.
We would have to know peace in order to want peace.

5.
When we learn how to become at peace within ourselves we will also be at peace with life.

6.
It is not what we have that gives us peace, but what we don't have that gives us peace.

7.
The more peaceful and quiet we are the more peaceful and quiet we'll become. Why is that so hard to do? As we are, we'll become.

8.
Peace and quiet: what a ponderous experience in life because the fine things in life are rare. What better gift could we give ourselves other than peace and quiet?

9.
Peace is not to concentrate on the qualities that make us most human, but to do the opposite because our natural purpose is also against any peacefulness.

10.
We never have everything we desire, but we can have peace and calm over ourselves.

11.
True greatness comes in the ability to see life clearly and to govern ourselves so as to become at peace.

12.
Peaceful is what we've needed all our lives, but didn't think about it.

13.
Wealth is for our desires and fears while wisdom is for peace and happiness.

14.
A mind at rest is as rare as it is fine to become peaceful and calm.

15.
Our highest authority over ourselves will result in calm and peace.

16.
All life is as it should be and always will be. We should know the only battles we'll ever have are within us. Our lives will become as peaceful as we can control ourselves.

17.
Peace and quiet was the reward of fleeing all that we ever desired or feared before.

18.
Pleasure is known by everybody, but peace is known by few. This is the difference between feeling and thinking.

19.
The end to our life's quest is to finally be at peace with ourselves. All of life has been the means to that end. This is done without knowing the quest.

20.
We accept a life we don't want to change, but we need to change a life we can't accept. When we are at peace with life, we don't want to change anything.

21.
We must long to become at peace within ourselves so each day will be its best. That peace can come at day's end, but all desire will never end.

22.
If we could have anything we wanted, isn't our peace of mind the most important?

23.
We don't get peace and quiet if we don't want peace and quiet.

24.
To think about thinking is our ultimate free will from what's controlling us and the reward is peace.

25.
No place to go or nothing to do is actually peace from ourselves, but we feel it's boring. That's the difference between thinking and feeling.

26.
Peace and quiet is boring when our feelings are as simplistic as that of a child.

27.
We are always seeking what's missing in our lives; we will never find peace when we're out of control.

28.
Peace and quiet is better than anything else, but we don't know this. It's why we're not in charge of ourselves.

29.
Our greatest possible success is when we have subdued the beast within in order to finally be peaceful and calm.

30.
We aren't happy because we want only pleasure, but that's just temporary. Happiness is a state of mind experienced when at peace with ourselves.

31.
Peace and quiet can be our life now, but it won' be easy or everyone would be there too.

32.
We are only as peaceful as to the degree of authority we have over ourselves.

33.
We get up in the morning and run like the wind all day. Why are we in such a hurry? We are just going to die without peace.

34.
We must know ourselves in order to be at peace with ourselves.

35.
Without demands from our ego, lust or fear come peace of mind.

36.
We must know not to listen to anyone or even ourselves if it doesn't make us peaceful and calm. Then it's just desire or fear.

37.
There is a peacefulness that comes over us when we know what is meaningful as opposed to what is not meaningful.

38.
Peace for me is happiness now, we are freed in the amount of influence we have from fact, truth, and reason.

39.
Be an island of peace in the storm of life by just not being the problem.

40.
Many may seek peace from the lives they made with alcohol or drugs, but there is no happiness in store like peace and calm.

41.
Boredom is the first step to finding peace and quiet.

42.
To be alone is happiness while pleasure is to be with others. We would not know this if we have not made the journey from social anxiety to become peaceful.

43.
Deliberate is peaceful and calm as the driver of our lives and not the driven.

44.
Our greatest good is the peace we can acquire for ourselves.

45.
Peace is from us, but pleasure is from others.

46.
Now I won, there is no place to go or nothing to do. That's our peace from ourselves; the rarest indeed are the finest things of all.

47.
When we are at peace within ourselves, we don't want anything else. Peace for me is happiness now.

48.
Peace and quiet is wonder filled or boring as determined by our thinking or feeling.

49.
Peace from within is heaven now.

50.
When we have few wants we gain much peace.

51.
Peace comes to those who want tranquility not pleasure.

52.
Peace is in knowing what we have and not what we want.

53.
When we follow our dreams they don't really matter if we don't find peace and quiet along the way.

54.
We may not know that peacefulness will make us happy.

55.
Finely it is so peaceful to live without desires, but no one else knows.

56.
We can't live for our fantasies and be peaceful and calm too.

57.
When we have peace within ourselves and with life, there is no desire to change.

58.
When we are at peace within ourselves, there is nothing that needs to be done except just live.

59.
When one makes peace within themselves they will also find happiness too.

60.
Peace from our desires and fears is realized when we have no place to go or nothing to do.

61.
To have more with less is a hard concept to realize.

62.
We can't improve on peace and calm if we thought about it.

63.
When we are finally peaceful and calm we have influence over ourselves.

64.
If heaven is to become peaceful, then we should learn to be now.

65.
Our peace from possessions and others will result in our peace from ourselves.

66.
Peace and quiet is rarely seen, but much less experienced, like this moment. It is sunrise now and I must go to experience it.

67.
We are running all the time or we are at peace with time.

68.
The best course in life is to become peaceful.

69.
What we need most, no one can give us, that's peace and quiet.

70.
We must know me, myself and I to finally become at peace within.

71.
The universe seems to be striving not to be at peace with itself, so our greatest accomplishment is to be at peace with ourselves too. Zero sum, net gain.

72.
Life can be so peaceful, but we are not.

73.
Let us be as one mentally within ourselves for peacefulness.

74.
Life should not be just fun and excitement, but peace is from us.

75.
Strive for peacefulness and we'll be happy.

76.
The truth is clear, but differs from our intentions. That's because peace from ourselves is happiness now.

77.
It can blow like hell out there in society, but it is peaceful and calm in here. Then we're in control of ourselves.

78.
Let go now or never know peace.

79.
Peace is our ability to become whole without contradiction.

80.
Let go instead of hold on more.

81.
When we get older we will just have more baggage unless we are at peace with ourselves.

82.
Peacefulness is the best of life.

83.
We are not finished until the last desire is hung.

84.
When we are peaceful, clear thinking is what's meaningful.

85.
Peace is the lack of fun or excitement.

86.
Peace from others is about peace from ourselves.

87.
Nothing controls us when we can control ourselves.

88.
Let go of all that we want all of the time. It has never been peaceful without us thinking. We've been on automatic controls and that's not beneficial.

89.
Peace is elusive to find because of us.

90.
Peace and quiet is a life we will never know if we don't stop to think about it.

91.
Let go if you can, but most cannot.

92.
Peace is freedom from desires while precious things are bondage to our emotions.

93.
When we gain possessions, we lose peace; so when we lose possessions, we gain peace. Therefore, the more we have the more we lose.

94.
Peace from ourselves is the third way from pleasure or pain all the time. When we know this we can become free from desires and fears.

95.
To become free we must control ourselves and peace is our reward.

96.
Peace and quiet is underrated; it's our freedom from oppressive emotions.

97.
Peace of mind is peace from ourselves.

98.
Peace of mind is the influence we have over ourselves.

99.
Peace from ourselves is well worth all we had to give up to acquire it.

100.
We must catch on in order to let go.

101.
Peacefulness is control of ourselves.

102.
Losers win and winners will lose because less is more and more is less. Our inaction is key to peace because peace is key to our happiness.

103.
Attachment to our restless roots is controlled by our stillness and calm.

104.
Life is a full glass running onto the floor.

105.
Know this, there is peace from ourselves.

106.
Life is blissful when we are peaceful and calm.

107.
There is nothing required to be added to or subtracted from our lives when we are peaceful.

108.
When life gets easier we are at peace with life, ourselves.

109.
When our best company is our own company, then we are at peace with life and ourselves.

110.
We may be running in the wrong direction if we are not thinking of peace.

111.
If we desire there may be pleasure, but if we want peace there is peacefulness.

112.
Peace and quiet is my old friend now at the end of my life.

113.
Loneliness is the price we pay for peace and quiet.

114.
When we are yielding we don't have to overcome the strong, they're not our equal any more.

115.
We have chosen all that we possess but if we are still unfulfilled then maybe we should have chosen to be still instead.

116.
There are others who will follow you easily when they realize you have won over yourself.

117.
Living a quiet life is hopeful and fulfilling, but living a busy life is hopeless and unfulfilling.

118.
When we acquired possessions we have risk of loss, but when we acquired experiences we are risk free.

119.
Desire requires actions, but tranquility requires inaction.

120.
We may not want to be free because it's not fun or exciting it's just peaceful and calm.

121.
When we empty our minds we are at peace and when we fill our minds we are resentful.

CHAPTER FOURTEEN

HARMONY:
Stop denying the truth

1.
Harmony is what remains when we stop denying the truth.

2.
When we relinquish possessions we will gain freedom for harmony. This comes from our higher thinking and not our lower desires.

3.
"At one" is harmony from our higher thinking over our lower instincts.

4.
Personal harmony is our heaven now at peace within us.

5.
Harmony with nature's laws that are within us are most difficult.

6.
Harmony is how lucky it is to have lived.

7.
Our harmony is mental unity for emotional and intellectual accord.

8.
When we don't strive to affect life or be affected much by life then we are harmonious with life and ourselves.

9.
All our lives are planned without actually thinking clearly or we would have achieved some degree of harmony in life by now.

10.
To have peace from ourselves is to know harmony within.

11.
When we realize all life is good we even like the bad, as it affects us very little.

12.
We'll find what we seek in the way life is and not as we wanted it to be.

13.
We are living the dream or chasing the fantasy. Harmony is the difference.

14.
If we were really free from our thoughts or could will our minds, wouldn't we choose to become peaceful, calm, tranquil, blissful and in harmony with life and ourselves?

15.
Peace and quiet is happiness to our highest thinking when we are in harmony within ourselves.

16.
Life gets better when we're kind to ourselves.

17.
Life is not confusing; it is us that made life confusing. We must figure ourselves out in order to live in harmony with life.

18.
When we are at peace within ourselves, we are at harmony with life too.

19.
Our harmony was the result of us arranging and interweaving of different internal forces into a single arrangement of calm and tranquility.

20.
Our quiet peace and tranquility is harmony between our mind's struggle for superiority.

21.
Harmony is our ultimate unity with heaven on earth.

22.
Fleeing is the passive way of life.

23.
What greater accomplishment than to be in harmony with life and ourselves?

24.
To restore friendship and agreement within our two minds is to become at one in harmony within ourselves.

25.
We come and then we must go, so being good is much more important than just feeling good.

26.
When we become in tune with life then life will become in tune with us.

27.
Harmony is our balance between emotional and higher thinking.

28.
We are the author of all our struggles.

29.
All that we add to our lives is also distracting; when we don't catch on we can't let go.

30.
We feel we know what's best, but superior knowledge is the path of least resistance.

31.

There is greatness in all of us when we stop to think and look, for we will only find what we seek.

32.

Now may be more important than anything else, but we may not know that.

33.

Find no fault with life, only with our ability to see life clearly.

34.

We tend to see life's imperfections and not life's many perfections.

35.

To be effective in our decisions is not a desired effect, but a permanent effect.

36.

Our harmony is happiness in heaven with life, then ourselves.

37.

Our life is what we seek.

38.

We have been here and we have been there, but nothing matters as much as the time spent in between.

39.

This is as good as it can get, but we don't live our lives as though it is. For now is better than yesterday or tomorrow, but that isn't where our minds like to live.

40.

When stillness of the very early morning matches the stillness of our mind, this can happen when we take the time.

41.

To know ourselves is to finally see life clearly, for we have always obstructed the best lessons of life.

42.
All our lives we still cannot see we are the problem and not the solution.

43.
To be in harmony is to be happy, to be happy is to be in heaven now.

44.
Rest is preferable to unrest, but we are indifferent to the unrest within us.

45.
To see ourselves clearly is its end within itself because all our confusion is what's confusing.

46.
Peacefulness in a life of confusion is our mind over feelings.

47.
We get obsessed by the details of our lives, but miss the reality of life.

48.
Our minds work for our good.

49.
When we are with another we can't be with ourselves. Oh, how we miss our insights when they are only out sights.

50.
Perfection is greater than all its parts, which is why it is beyond our grasp. We are not whole until we figure that out.

51.
Our mind has the ability to understand and express humanity's essence to us as we relate to life.

52.
"0" sum gain is the balance between emotions and wisdom.

53.
Harmony is found in the authority we have over ourselves.

54.
I'm happier without desire, aren't you?

55.
By stilling our desires we will still our minds.

56.
Moral excellence is contentment and happiness.

57.
Time disturbs or rests the mind; this was our choice.

58.
When nothing is desired we aren't compelled any more.

59.
We must acquire self-control in order to possess self-respect and self-sufficiency.

60.
We will own things or we will own ourselves.

61.
We know many who are looking for all things but few of them who are in harmony.

62.
Harmony is our will over nature's will for a zero net gain.

63.
When we're not working for recognition anymore we'll have much more free time to live.

64.
Without awe of life we will just go back to work again today.

65.
When we compete we will be meet with competition, but when we welcome we will be meet with generosity.

66.
We will come to great harm if we don't know our enemy lies within.

67.
Ambition is a course to oppose others in order to win, but in harmony we have won already.

68.
When we act on all that is beneficial and reject all that is not, we are in harmony.

69.
Our lives are spent on all that we acquired; maybe our lives were too much to spend so foolishly.

70.
Activity brings disorder but stillness brings tranquility.

71.
We all know the value of actions but seem not to know the value of inaction.

72.
One must remain at one with oneself to know the unknown peace, rest and happiness.

73.
We are free without possessions and homeless, for contentment is indifferent to all things.

74.
Our success is realized by encountering the least resistance in life.

75.
A passive person can overcome life's challenges because they resist effortlessly.

76.
A wise person has gained self-restraint in all things and is rewarded with contentment.

CHAPTER FIFTEEN

SIMPLICITY:
Our greatness is simplicity

1.
There is greatness in simplicity because non-action is easy and rewarded with little, while action is difficult and rewarded with much.

2.
Life is simple so we must have a simple life too, but most make life complicated and aren't happy either.

3.
When we do not know what to do then doing nothing is an option too.

4.
A simple life is the life to be or we may never have thought to see.

5.
Less is more must be the best kept secret in our world.

6.
Loneliness is our friend; poverty is peaceful, quiet for the simplicity. Life is without desire or fear. Our freedom from all things is found within ourselves.

7.
We must be looking for the path of least resistance in order to find one.

8.
It requires a simplistic lifestyle in order to think more clearly. Ignoring others' complicating factors frees us from pretense and guile by reducing our life to its basic essence.

9.
When we hurry we lose and when we slow down we gain.

10.
Loneliness is the reality of a simple life.

11.
Simplicity is the effect of wisdom.

12.
It is easier to let go than it is to hold on.

13.
The less we want is the more we'll have.

14.
More feels there is something missing while less is to know there is more.

15.
We can't serve two motivations, for a divided mind can't stand alone. One is a task master while the other is a lazy friend.

16.
Let the games begin, everyone wants to play but does not know that fleeing is an option rarely seen and much less taken.

17.
When we give up everything we have nothing to lose and have won ourselves life.

18.
The simple life is the life to be, does no one else want to be free and happy?

19.
When we don't want anything, we don't have anything and that's a simple life.

20.
Less is more, but we must have less to know.

21.
The simple life is the life for the free from vanity and deceit, that's me.

22.
More is less or less is more?

23.
We limit our outlook by always looking inward to our individual self-interests. By keeping our goals to a minimum we embrace external reality.

24.
Life is for the experiences and not for the possessions.

25.
When we think of simplicity we will find happiness.

26.
To become the best we can perceive is our simplistic detachment.

27.
To accomplish the most difficult would be to take life easy.

28.
We must catch on in order to let go.

29.
The homeless life is simplistic and free.

30.
Society can't defeat someone who isn't really participating.

31.
Nothing asked or nothing given of myself is a free moment to be happy.

32.
When we require little is a gift to ourselves.

33.
Those whom have much are depleted and those who have little are replenished.

34.
We need to learn how to let go because we already know how to hold on.

35.
What we want from others will take cunning, but what we need for ourselves will be simple.

36.
The obvious has escaped our attention, that is, when we acquire more we are less happy.

37.
When less and less is achieved more and more is possible.

38.
We will learn more with less because we will get a life to live.

39.
Know as much as you can but do as little as possible, know all things but have few things, learn by the example of others of what not to do.

40.
There is success in very little in order to enjoy life to the fullest.

41.
Understanding comes from being open to life. To do little is nourishing; we can take credit for not being dominated by life's demands.

CHAPTER SIXTEEN

FREEDOM:
Controlled by our unknown

1.
We think we are free because we know what we want, but all our wants are for the same things. There is little freedom in being controlled by our unknown.

2.
It has taken us a lifetime to get where we are. Yet we aren't free. When freedom is not our goal then bondage is all we reap.

3.
When we use our higher thinking life becomes much clearer. How could we have not seen ourselves, life in this way? Give up struggling today so we can be free tomorrow. A life of our own making.

4.
The course of our lives is by destiny of emotional motivations or designed by higher thinking. That is without or with free will.

5.
The power of our feelings makes slaves of us all. The influence of our mind over our feelings makes us free from ourselves.

6.
When we are the freest, we are least like ourselves.

7.
Our failure was to prohibit or enforce authority over ourselves in order to be free.

8.
We may have been better off to have never done anything that everyone else is doing because no one else seems to be free from their choices.

9.
The more we have the more we want, but the less we have the less we want.

10.
When we know the laws of nature over our life, we can finally control what controls us in order to become free.

11.
Bondage is movement toward our desires and away from our fears. Freedom is movement toward our fears and away from our desires.

12.
We become free when we know ourselves, but are enslaved when we don't.

13.
We all desire to be enslaved or we would be free.

14.
Suffering is our mind made prisoner. To become free we must know this.

15.
Attachment is subjection to compulsion and the lack of freedom to determine one's course of action and condition of living.

16.
When we are most free we are least ourselves.

17.
We are only free when we know how to be, otherwise we are just as we are now.

18.
A free life is without attachment or commitment.

19.
When we are free from ourselves there is no place to go or nothing that needs to be done.

20.
Pleasure serves us for such a short while, but we serve desires for pleasure all of our lives. Who's free from themselves and know this now, is their own master.

21.
We feel we must have free choice because we know what we desire, but the cause of our motivations is actually unknown to us because we're not thinking.

22.
When we are truly free we will know it, but when we are not free we will not know it.

23.
Free time is more important than money because now is more important than yesterday or tomorrow.

24.
Freedom from us is owning less so less owns us, for less stress and anxiety is more clam and tranquil.

25.
To become free, we must control what controls us; that is our ego, lust, fear (money, sex, time).

26.
Our minds are a sanctuary or a prison by our choices; we are free or not free.

27.
We are all driven but not the driver and until we know this we will not be free.

28.
We must want to become free from ourselves before we will become freed.

29.
When we do not want anything, then we are free to do anything we want.

30.
We wish and desire freely, but yet we are not free to think.

31.
We must think in order to be happy and feel to have pleasure. When we are free to think we are peaceful and calm.

32.
We are motivated by our bodies; this knowledge alone will set our minds free from our senses controlling us all our lives.

33.
All our time and money is spent on desires for pleasure, but we still feel we are free.

34.
Our cerebral cortex is our highest thinking, not our desires or fears of our senses, for our true freedom is away from our lowest feelings.

35.
When we choose to have less then less has us and we are free to become free.

36.
Slackers are underrated for carefree is free to care.

37.
When life controls us, we don't control our lives; if we did we would be free now.

38.
We must resent authority to have authority over ourselves.

39.
The freedom to be me is not to be controlled by me.

40.
Those who have the least are free to be themselves.

41.
Life could be freeing, but we'll never know we are controlled by what controls us without having even a choice.

42.
Freedoms are lost because we don't know freedom from ourselves.

43.
We have reached a promised place when we are free from ourselves. We were always the problem so must become our own solution.

44.
We must know what freedom is from ourselves before we are free.

45.
We feel we are free when we know what we want by striving for all that we may feel is fun, but we aren't free when we can't control what we think.

46.
Personal freedom is the sole responsibility of the individual.

47.
We are never free from ourselves if we don't even try. We are simply embracing our flaws.

48.
Our highest state is freedom from ourselves; by becoming the master of ourselves is without us always striving.

49.
We are troubled by what is troubling us, yet we can't see this clearly in order to become free.

50.
Freedom is to self-determine one's course of action and conditions of living.

51.
If everyone is controlled by what controls them, then they are not free.

52.
We are not free till the last weakness is hung.

53.
Life is working best for us is when we're not working for life.

54.
We will not be free until we know the cause of our wishes and desires.

55.
Maturity is our final stage of life without obligations.

56.
A person who is free from the desires for wealth or fears of loss possesses little, but has it all figured out.

57.
To become free we must just be the boss of ourselves and nobody else.

58.
When we know ourselves we become free.

59.
When we are free, we can control who we are because we are the problem or its solution. Look no farther than the mirror to see who we really are.

60.
Nothing can control us when we control ourselves.

61.
When we're addicted to addictions that are pleasurable that's all that controls us. Then we are not free.

62.
The only freedom we will ever have is the authority we have over ourselves in order to control what is controlling us.

63.
We are only as free as much as we are free from ourselves.

64.
Desire and fear is something we must do, but peace and quiet is something we must want to do. This is the way of a deliberate life, to choose freedom over bondage.

65.
Know the value of a slacker for non-action has value too.

66.
When we are controlled by what controls us, we are not free to think.

67.
The easy life is the hardest to live without thinking.

68.
Our lives should be a free choice and not what we feel we should do.

69.
To just let go is the hardest endeavor, but the most liberating.

70.
The tighter we hold on the more we are held.

71.
We are looking for what we like the most, but the less we own the less owns us.

72.
If we don't let go we will always be just hanging on.

73.
To share life with someone else becomes a distraction of life's experiences. It's for their wellbeing and not our own.

74.
When our minds are open all things become possible without even knowing what they may be: the birth of imagination outside of our current self-imposed limitations.

75.
We must let go of what controls us in order to become free.

76.
When we are free from ourselves can we know absolute freedom?

77.
The less that we possess is the less that we are possessed by.

78.
Trying too hard is what is the matter.

79.
We will become liberated when we stop our emotional decisions.

80.
Imagination is the freedom to think out loud.

81.
To flee from oneself is to be free from ourselves.

82.
To leave our limitations behind us we just have to do what we haven't been doing.

83.
To have power over oneself is sublime freedom.

84.
To become free makes one want to remain free.

85.
All we have learned didn't that make us free because more bondage is all we learned.

86.
Want to be free tomorrow then just don't do what you did today.

87.
We will gain freedom and happiness at the expense of possessions and positions.

88.
When we decided to work without recondition or money we can do anything we want, because when work without gain we are working for our interests and no others.

89.
To have little control over others means we have learned to have great control over ourselves; for advantages over others is also a disadvantage to ourselves.

90.
Detachment is indifference to others' concerns and freedom from attachment.

91.
We don't know who our master is or that we could even be master of our own fate. We have been broken by society at an early age in submission to desires and fears.

92.
Prime time is our time alone.

93.
Time spent alone is our gift from "wisdom of the ages."

94.
When one realizes that all we may have sought was meaningless, we are reborn free.

CHAPTER SEVENTEEN

ALONE:
To become all-one

1.
We must be alone to become all-one. That's wisdom of the ages.

2.
The hardest thing to accept when we acquire happiness is to be alone. This is the path least traveled: to be at one with ourselves and nature.

3.
Our privacy is worth more than anything else for our mind's depths are only approachable after many days and years of solitude.

4.
What a special place, to be with ourselves in solitude, for peace of mind is being a best friend to ourselves.

5.
To live alone by choice and not necessity is the result of our wisdom.

6.
When we prefer to be alone than with anyone else, we are contented or crazy.

7.
When we learn that solitude will give us happiness we know what we have is more than what we want from others or possessions.

8.
Solitude affords the time required to have wisdom from reason and logic, that's not to be found outside of us.

9.

Those who have been alone for many years know what most can never know, that is themselves.

10.

When it is better to be alone than it is to be with others, we are happy, contented and wise.

11.

The more we want from others, the more they want from us. The more we are alone, the more we want to be alone.

12.

When we are alone it is easier to see our desires and fears, so as to become capable of living a deliberate life.

13.

Living along in a cave and being happy is better than living in a castle and not being happy.

14.

To be alone we have to know and like ourselves; but in order to know ourselves we have to be alone.

15.

That we have to be alone to see life clearly is why so few can see life clearly.

16.

Life doesn't get any better than to be alone in nature at peace with life and ourselves.

17.

What is limiting our thinking is that the road less traveled is lonely all the way.

18.

Seclusion is not a desire for pleasure or fear of pain.

19.
How can we ever expect to want to be alone with ourselves if we don't know, like, or respect ourselves?

20.
Solitude is not only to be found in a cave because it can be anywhere; we separate our mind from our desires and fears.

21.
Few can still their emotions in order to become peaceful and quiet. We must be alone in order to be happy.

22.
All possessions or achievements are for the pleasures received from others, because alone they are unimportant.

23.
We have to learn how to be at peace with life and ourselves so we may know freedom to be alone and contented with who we have become.

24.
Fellowship is pleasure with others. Then mellowship is happiness alone.

25.
It is really easy to be alone, but the hardest part is to actually like it.

26.
Up and up into our higher thinking we must climb all alone, that is why some never venture.

27.
Alone in our thoughts we will find we're really not alone. This is the hidden truth so few have found, but is there for everyone to discover.

28.
When we are alone, we can do what we think and not just what feels good with others.

29.

When we are by ourselves is when we learn about ourselves.

30.

When we are alone a lot, it seems like we're with an old friend we spent our whole lives with and we have gotten to know, like.

31.

The path less traveled is time we spend all alone. Peacefulness and quiet is free.

32.

We are happier to live alone, but we have more pleasure to live with others.

33.

It is good to be alone because it forces us to think.

34.

To separate from others is to obtain a pure free state of a quiet life in a place of seclusion.

35.

To be alone is the influence of our mind over the power of our bodies.

36.

When we can live alone, then we can also be happy.

37.

To be with others is desire and satisfaction of our senses, but to be alone is for peace of mind over our instincts.

38.

Peace and quiet is being alone with ourselves. Why do we feel this is so bad? (We are not thinking.)

39.

To isolate ourselves from others we will gain a pure free state without equal.

40.
The time we spend alone in thought will turn out to be time well spent.

41.
A higher state of mind governed by reason and logic is to be alone in nature without desire or fear.

42.
The times we spend alone are the best times of our lives, when we know and respect ourselves.

43.
Quiet solitude is our friend. Those who don't know friendship within don't have peace of mind. To be your best friend is better than being your worst enemy.

44.
Through our instincts and intelligence there is a hopeless narrative. It's that we must be alone in time in order that we may develop a capacity for wisdom.

45.
Solitude is peace from our desires and fears.

46.
Time spent alone thinking has the greatest value because it is consciousness, peace and happiness.

47.
A mind that is not troubled by itself is happy.

48.
To be alone a lot we start to like the peace and quiet.

49.
Being alone is to control what controls us, our harmony will exist over our ego, lust and fear.

50.
We must run from others in order to find ourselves.

51.
Alone is all-one, a peaceful, tranquil, quiet answer to life.

52.
To be alone in nature is our happiest time: to know life and ourselves.

53.
We must be alone to become all-one, because all-one within us is happiness.

54.
We must be a-lone in order to be all-one with ourselves. We will not know this when we are always with someone else.

55.
We may not desire this, but our isolation is the key to success for a pure free state.

56.
Our self-isolation and subjective experiences are without anxiety, guilt, dread or anguish.

57.
Nothing is better than to be alone and know it. That's peace now for us, from us.

58.
It must be lonely to be wise for so few go to the farthest reaches of their minds.

59.
When in danger and doubt we must go away in order to figure life out.

60.
We must stand alone to become free from ourselves.

61.
To be alone and like it is a success because it is not pleasurable, but is happiness.

62.
We need to be alone to think and we need to be with others to not think.

63.
We must go backward into ourselves in order to find ourselves.

64.
Alone for a meaningful life of happiness by thinking, and not just feelings that turn to turmoil and despair.

65.
To be alone is prime time when we think about it.

66.
Our isolation is a self-imposed vacuum for a stillness in order to see us and life more clearly.

67.
We must be alone to be happy or with others for pleasure.

68.
Life is calmer alone than it is with others.

69.
We cannot be peaceful with someone.

70.
It is great to be alone except it is lonely. We may feel this, but we don't think this.

71.
We must live alone for the peace and respect our lives deserve.

72.
Alone is all-one as a whole within us.

73.
To live with anyone is not going to be fair. We would have to give up our identity in order to share.

74.
When we are with someone we always take away from ourselves.

75.
To be with anyone is inhibiting.

76.
Life is a journey alone even though there are friends, family and loved ones around us.

77.
The homeless state is the end to our desires and fears as nonsense. Now is drifting and smiling, but before wasn't knowing better. Others have needs, but alone we have nothing to need.

78.
Alone, but not lonely, within our higher thinking.

79.
When we're lonely, we can be happy. Because considering we are behind, we are ahead.

80.
We can't stand to be alone because it is not fun or exciting.

81.
Friday night is a special time, that's when we party with ourselves for the week is done, but we are not.

82.
We are missing ourselves when we're not alone.

83.
When prime time is being alone, we are at peace with ourselves when living unlimited by the restraints of desire and fear.

84.
It is a sad life if we don't make time to be alone.

85.
It is really lonelier to be in a big city than to be in the desert by ourselves, because in a big city we miss being alone by ourselves.

86.
When we think about life and ourselves, we will be alone.

87.
We seem to be in such a hurry to get through life quickly we can't ever get to know ourselves along the way.

88.
To all those who have lived alone, solitude is a boon, not boring.

89.
Alone is not lonely if coupled with reason and logic, because all-one is meaningful.

90.
To really live is to be left alone by others.

91.
Our successes don't require others for mutual pleasure, but must be done alone to be secured within ourselves.

92.
A time to know time is time alone.

93.
When we're alone we have the opportunity to be happy if we think about it. Thinking about it will make the difference.

94.
The best company we can acquire is ourselves.

95.
When we accept ourselves we will accept others less.

96.
Alone is all-one within our thinking and feelings.

97.
Stillness and quiet is our friend and not an enemy.

98.
We must isolate ourselves in order to think clearly.

99.
Life is something very special when we are alone so we can think.

100.
There is an awareness we may not experience if we are not alone without outside interferences.

101.
Sunrise and sunset are the greatest times to be alone.

102.
When we resign from our life as we know it, we have shed the old to have the new.

103.
When we're still and alone early in the morning with just our thoughts of the moment, this is not only rare but the greatest times of our lives.

104.
Alone with our thoughts is a communion with all thinkers. Alone, just let go, you're safe within yourself.

105.
The idea that we have to be alone to become happy goes unknown.

106.
Time spent alone can be well spent.

107.
Consciousness of ourselves and life can be known alone.

108.
The company of others is stressful, but solitude is peaceful and quiet.

109.
Learn to be alone or be unhappy with pleasure.

110.
We require others for pleasure, but require solitude for happiness.

111.
We need solitude for thinking or others for feelings.

112.
The knowledge gained while alone without social or religious biases is free thinking.

113.
When we're alone we can learn to like ourselves, or if we like ourselves we are alone.

114.
We will have to look long and hard to find the calmness between our thoughts for the most special time is to be alone and happy with our mind.

115.
We can all be happy but it's a learned response and not a natural response.

CHAPTER EIGHTEEN

HAPPINESS:
Give up desire to have happiness

1.
Nothing is more unpleasant than not having what we desire. Nothing is happier than not desiring at all. That we must give up desire to have happiness seems counterintuitive, but works.

2.
We don't know what we don't know is why we are not happy.

3.
There is a stillness in happiness, so we must still ourselves to find it.

4.
Pain is our lack of pleasure or happiness, but our happiness is the lack or desire that causes pain.

5.
We must go within us for solutions to be happy or outside of ourselves to get pleasure. This is to be or to do.

6.
We seem to prefer any and all beliefs that will give us pleasure as opposed to any possibility of our happiness.

7.
For pleasure we must pay for the amount due, but for happiness is the credit that we must give to ourselves.

8.
Isn't our greatest success found not in the control over others for pleasure, but control over ourselves for happiness?

9.

Free will is suspect to our inability to choose between alternatives of pleasure and happiness. Thus we are never happy.

10.

To become distrustful of our motives is the reality that the worst possible outcome is we aren't ever going to be happy.

11.

Our happiness is the result of actively engaging the creative use of our intellect for kindness and gentleness to ourselves.

12.

Our quality of life is the opposite of our standard of living. One is a mental, the other is physical. True happiness is a mental state of mind, but standard of living isn't.

13.

We must divorce pleasure in order to marry happiness.

14.

We are all living the life of our fantasy, but our choices weren't for peace, quiet, calm, tranquility, bliss or harmony, or we would be happy now in our dreams.

15.

To have to give up so much so as to have so little and be so happy is all our choices: Wealth or wisdom, pleasure or happiness, fear or peace and heaven or hell.

16.

Our desire for pleasure results in turmoil, confusion and agitation, while happiness is calm, tranquil and undisturbed.

17.

We shouldn't allow pleasure to have us at the exclusion of free will to become happy. This isn't an unrealizable goal, but a choice when there was none.

18.

We can't have both happiness and pleasure at the same time for one is mental awareness and the other is simplistic feelings and wishful rationalizations.

19.

All life's struggle because nature wills its course through us without us knowing. Until we know this, we can never will our own happiness.

20.

The path of least resistance most often turns out to be best for our happiness, but worse for desire and fear.

21.

We are so busy seeking our desires and dealing with our fears, we can't see life clearly. We would be much better off doing nothing as trying to do everything and still not being happy.

22.

Greatness is influence over ourselves; for happiness and not power over others for pleasure. When we know this, we are free from ourselves.

23.

A deliberate life is one in which we know what's best for happiness and not what's just for pleasure.

24.

We do all we desire for pleasure yet we are never peaceful and calm, blissful and harmonious, which is happiness. Think now and not be fooled anymore.

25.

We must fight for our pleasures and we must flee for our happiness. This shows us how our two minds work.

26.

Life is nature's way all the way from cradle to grave. There is just one slim hope that we can know ourselves along the way to become happy.

27.

Our gaze is past, over, through any happiness we could possibly experience now for just a glimpse of pleasure in a distant unsure future.

28.

Although we all knew what we wanted, then why weren't we very happy with it when we got it?

29.

Stop, look and listen: you're not going the right way if you're not happy now! Tomorrow never comes, yesterday is past. Now I won, it is time and place I dwell and abide.

30.

Where happiness dwells and abides is now, but we may not know because it is not fun or exciting.

31.

When we can still our fears and desires, we become peaceful and calm. This freedom from ourselves is happiness now.

32.

If all we have is peace and quiet, that's more than anyone else will ever have. Think on this and be happy.

33.

There is nothing more contented than to be happy, but no one else is trying to become peaceful and calm.

34.

As children we trusted all those in our lives to know what was best for us. They taught us pleasure and not how to be happy.

35.

How could we ever have thought we would be happy by always doing what everyone else wants us to do for them, when they're not happy either?

36.

All that we can see and do yet not to know true happiness, because we must let go of ego, lust and fear.

37.

We must work all of our lives for desires of ego, lust or fear of loss, but we don't have to work at all for peace and happiness, that's conscious of life and our self.

38.

Life is for the mind or life is for the body. We all have made that choice between pleasure or happiness. One is thinking, while the other is emotion.

39.

Through a creative process of our upper level of mental awareness and the discipline to forget our own fleeting desire for pleasures, we can gain the ultimate happiness.

40.

Our happiness must be a free choice and is not our instinctive motivation.

41.

Pleasure is confirmed in the proof that our standard of living is far more important to us than our happiness, that's quality of life.

42.

Our refusal to admit the truth of reality will result in us trying to satisfy our desires all our lives without ever being happy.

43.

We must admit life is not clearer than at the beginning, but with increasing wisdom comes our ability to direct us away from what's troubling us toward a happier life.

44.

We should listen to what we don't want to hear instead of what we want to hear. That is the reason we have never been happy. The choices we made were not peaceful or calm as they could be.

45.

The problem is all stress and anxieties are found in our desires or fears. The problem's solution is peace from ourselves in order to become happy.

46.
All of our addictions, compulsions, desires and fears will always take precedence over any ability to become happy by thinking.

47.
Others may give us pleasure, but only we can give ourselves happiness. That's our mind over our body.

48.
When anyone likes being alone, peaceful and quiet, they will be happy too. We are in control of others for pleasure, and ourselves for happiness.

49.
We will not find happiness if we're always looking for pleasure.

50.
Leaving our societies of ego, lust and fear to a simpler security in nature is peace, joy and happiness.

51.
Postponing our happiness is just foolishness because life will become burdensome and nothing will be liberating.

52.
You have a house, you have a mate, you have a job, you have a religion, but you are not happy yet?

53.
Give up so much, have so little and be so happy.

54.
Our greatness is our ability to gain wisdom and its application in our lives, this would result in peace from our desires and fears in order to become happy.

55.
When we know what we want, we're distracted from what we could have now. That's life, liberty and the pursuit of happiness. Pleasure is a poor substitute for true happiness.

56.
When we decrease our desires we will increase our happiness at the same rate.

57.
We are without a doubt the most misunderstood by ourselves. Otherwise, we would be happy and well-adjusted now. Other than wise is who we are now.

58.
Money will give us some of the pleasures we desire, but not all of them. When we are happy we don't think of desire or money.

59.
What we are always seeking doesn't make us happy or everyone would be happy. Then why do we seek if it doesn't make us happy?

60.
We live for pleasure, but feel we have to die to be happy. (Religion)

61.
We will always feel we want more until we know we can't trust our feelings anymore.

62.
Quietness is self-empowering because peace from ourselves is happiness now.

63.
Here's to us and all that looking around because we are only as far as we were unhappy and thought it could be better.

64.
In order to be happy, we have to do what no one else is willing to do because no one else is happy. Heaven is now, if we think about it.

65.
Our greatest accomplishment in life is to become peaceful, calm and happy with ourselves and all of life.

66.

We are just a decision away from being happy, but the vividness of our desires and fears will always take it away.

67.

The easiest, shortest way to become happy is to want less.

68.

The more money we have the more pleasure we have, but the less happy we are.

69.

Free time or money is a core belief for pleasure or happiness.

70.

Peace is controlling what controls us. Joy is in possessing what gives us happiness all the days of our lives.

71.

Happiness is our life without illusions.

72.

Everyone is his own gate keeper. Happiness is harmony within us. Bliss is not wanting anything or anybody, at peace. When we're happy, we don't want anything.

73.

Do you remember when you didn't have much and you were the happiest?

74.

If we were not happy yesterday and we're just doing the same things today, then we probably won't be happy tomorrow either.

75.

When we know how to be happy, we will find we have to be alone because when we're with others we will find we have to do what pleases them in order to have pleasure.

76.

We either go from cradle to grave in the fastest time possible in pursuit of our desires or the slowest time possible in pursuit of happiness.

77.

Happiness is dependent on our current state of mind as reflected by our decisions; it is what we bring to now that's either baggage or bliss.

78.

We must give up pleasure in order to become happy. We don't feel that will feel good and it won't.

79.

If we are always thinking about desires or pleasures we can't be happy. We can only have one thought at a time. Just think don't feel and be happy.

80.

All pleasures decrease our happiness, this is why so few are happy.

81.

You'll know when you are happy because you'll think you're in heaven.

82.

When we have pleasure we miss happiness and when we have happiness we miss pleasure. This is our two minds feeling and thinking.

83.

Happiness is in owning ourselves, while pleasure is to be owned by others or possessions.

84.

Desire is too much trouble when we think about it, but happiness is no trouble at all.

85.
Harmony is heaven here or maybe in some other far off, distant place in another life; or maybe it is just time to become happy here and now.

86.
Happiness is sustainable, but pleasure is not.

87.
We use our intellect as a power over others for pleasure or influence over us for happiness.

88.
Happiness is the freedom to determine ones course without desire or fear.

89.
We serve others for our pleasures or we serve our self for happiness. What's freedom or bondage?

90.
We have two minds, which is why we are unaware of the cause of our conflict. This is pleasure and happiness.

91.
We will never find happiness when we are always looking for pleasure.

92.
"Peace from Me is Happiness Now." We are the problem so we have to become our own solution because nobody or nothing can do it for us. That's happiness in for happiness out.

93.
We have two separate minds. One is emotions or feelings for pleasure or pain, the other is reason and logic or thinking for happiness, that's peace and calm.

94.
When we fear the loss of life and possessions, we can't know true happiness.

95.
Happiness seems to be most often associated with experiences in nature.

96.
It would take our greatest strengths in order to give up our greatest pleasure. It would take our greatest weaknesses to give up our greatest happiness.

97.
Pleasure is detrimental to happiness, but happiness is detrimental to pleasure. We feel to have pleasure, but must think to have happiness.

98.
Happiness is our upper level of mental life as contrasted by pleasure which is our lower level of mental life.

99.
When we are young we want to experience pleasure, but when we are mature we want to experience happiness.

100.
We always have desire. That is why we never have happiness.

101.
One who favors restricting themselves will maximize their happiness.

102.
Peace and quiet vs fun and excitement; the choice was easy. That's just why no one is happy.

103.
Life's greatness was in the best experiences and our highest awareness. When we make that happen we will be happy.

104.
True freedom will come when we are free from ourselves: know this to become happy.

105.
Standard of living is our lower feelings for pleasure, but quality of life is our higher thinking for happiness.

106.
Happiness realization was from our higher thinking and not our emotions of pleasure or pain.

107.
It is hard to be happy when we're trying to have fun all the time.

108.
The results of our decisions are meaningless if we are not happy now.

109.
Boring is our lack of fun and excitement. After boring will come peace and calm. One gives us desire while the other gives us happiness.

110.
All happiness is hidden just beyond what's boring, which is why we may not have been looking there.

111.
We can't give happiness to another. We can only give pleasure or pain because happiness is the truth that we must find for ourselves.

112.
When we're running around all our lives seeking gratification, we will never know ourselves enough to be happy.

113.
All happiness was the result of restraint exercised over one's own impulses, emotions and desires.

114.
If we only knew what was missing in our lives, we would know happiness now.

115.
Bosses have authority over others for their pleasure or influence over themselves for happiness.

116.
If we really wanted to become happy, we would have to stop doing what we've been doing before.

117.
Happiness is the highest state of mind when we're not troubled by desires for pleasure or fear of pain.

118.
We've got everything to be happy, we just don't know how to live like a beggar and walk like a king (Buddha).

119.
To be average is the problem because average people we know aren't happy, we must excel.

120.
We may hurry in the pursuit of pleasure and time. Slowing down in the pursuit of happiness will afford us a lot more time.

121.
Our knowledge and education are motivations for pleasure or fear of pain and not for happiness.

122.
We have power to have power over ourselves, and peace and quiet brings it out best. When we are free to be ourselves we are happy.

123.
The greatest knowledge is just to rule over ourselves, for we rule over others for pleasure or rule over ourselves for happiness.

124.
All that's important is our life, liberty, and happiness.

125.
Our knowledge is for the power to give us pleasures, while wisdom is influence over our self so as to become happy.

126.
The more pleasures we give up, the more happiness we acquire.

127.
We are defenseless of ourselves and life, but don't know this otherwise we would be happy now.

128.
All happiness is our mental reward for withstanding desire and fear. This is from our influence over ourselves.

129.
While always looking for pleasure we'll never find happiness because we don't even know what happiness is.

130.
Happiness isn't found in possessions or others, but within our consciousness of life so as to direct ourselves toward what is meaningful and away from what's meaningless.

131.
When not seeking happiness within us, we seek pleasure in all that we must do.

132.
We will have happiness by stilling our desires for pleasure.

133.
When we don't want to change anything in our lives we are content.

134.
Happiness will come to those who have thought about their motives.

135.
We can only give others pleasure, we can't give them happiness. That comes from within us.

136.

Our peace from the constant desire for pleasure will give us happiness.

137.

The freedom from ourselves is our happiness now and is life's greatest secret.

138.

We seek all that is pleasurable outside of us, but our happiness can only come from within.

139.

It is not easy to be happy. Otherwise everyone would be, but then what's most valuable is always the rarest too.

140.

When we know what we have now is much more important than what we may acquire in the future, we are contented and happy.

141.

We surrender our happiness to the power of others' pleasures or fears over us.

142.

When we are with others and miss being alone, we know that happiness is to become peaceful, calm, tranquil, blissful, harmonious and heavenly.

143.

Quality of life is happiness, but standard of living is pleasure.

144.

We may work all our life's long days without ever knowing happiness, which is only found by working less.

145.

We all know what desire is from birth till death, but we will not know what happiness is all our lives.

146.
When we aren't happy with ourselves, we won't be happy with life.

147.
To become free we must be less like who we are now. Our freedom is for us to become happy.

148.
Happiness, peace and joy is not for tomorrow, but now.

149.
We can't make others happy. We can only give them what they desire; our happiness is a state of mind that comes from within.

150.
What good are our motives if we are not happy?

151.
We will never know happiness if we never know ourselves.

152.
Fame and fortune is gained from pleasing others, but happiness is acquired from knowing ourselves.

153.
Happiness is when we are in control of ourselves.

154.
Happiness is found in the avoidance of desire and fear.

155.
We are a secret to ourselves because at the end of our day we have to like ourselves in order to be happy.

156.
Happiness is never the result of doing what we feel was good.

157.
Happiness is defeated by a desire for pleasure.

158.
To be human is not to be happy for unhappiness is much more human than happiness.

159.
We have to want to be happy more than fulfill our desires in order to think for ourselves.

160.
What good are our minds if we don't use them enough to become happy?

161.
We want to have pleasure for a while, but we should want happiness for a lifetime.

162.
Greater intelligence acquires more pleasure, but less happiness.

163.
Pleasure is what feels good while happiness is the result of our thinking.

164.
If we are not happy now why would we feel that more of the same could ever make us happy?

165.
When we are conscious of our mind's thinking, we are happier than when we are just feeling good.

166.
We don't have time to be happy because we are always looking for pleasure.

167.
When we are contented with happiness we will be with others less for our mutual pleasure.

168.
We must make wise decisions to be happy since we don't have to think to have pleasure.

169.
In order to be happy we must do what we think and not what we feel for pleasure.

170.
We have all thought what will give us pleasure, but not what will make us happy.

171.
Everyone knows how to have pleasure, but very few know how to be happy.

172.
Pleasure is with one's possessions and status is for respect from others, but our happiness is limiting our requirements and actions.

173.
Power over others for pleasure or influence over ourselves for happiness?

174.
Happiness is not always seeking pleasure. We are freed when we know what is controlling us. That is for us and not for others.

175.
Happiness is controlling what controls us, that is us.

176.
The absolute truth will give us the purpose to find happiness.

177.
When we get past bored that is where happiness dwells and abides.

178.
Happiness is a state of well-being, contentment and not controlled by our desires of societies that result in our suffering.

179.
Happiness is wisdom's reward.

180.
The absence of desire or fear is the way to know happiness.

181.
We seek pleasure but expect to be happy in return; only peace from our desires and fears will make us happy now.

182.
Let it all go and be happy now because it is not worth it if it didn't make you happy yesterday.

183.
Now is the time to be happy and not when we get what we're currently striving for, because now is the best time of our life except we don't know it.

184.
Happiness is a state of mind; by avoiding desire we acquire that state. Few will be able to know this because so few will ever try.

185.
We are always the problem of our unhappiness, which is our desire and fear.

186.
Happiness is just to be calm, tranquil. Isn't that better than anything else?

187.
Our happiness is not where we are at in life, but where our minds are at now.

188.
Desire and fear is all that stands between us and happiness.

189.
When life is difficult, then we are not doing it right.

190.
When we've learned to limit ourselves, it's a straight connection to our happiness.

191.
We all know pleasure very well. Then why don't we know how to be happy?

192.
Our happiness is a state of wellbeing through internal calm and tranquility, thus we are contented.

193.
Our natural cause is desire for pleasure, but our own thinking cause is for happiness.

194.
When we give others pleasure, that's diverting us from our own happiness.

195.
When we take charge of our self, that's our consciousness of desire and fear for the freedom to become happy.

196.
Since we're always looking for pleasure, we won't find happiness.

197.
The life we live should be the best we can make it, so we may be as happy as possible for as long as we have.

198.
To resolve to become happy in paradise now is not easy or everyone would be happy now.

199.
When we are in control, we will know, but it will not be easy or everybody would be happy.

200.

While knowing what we want gives us pleasure, then knowing what we have gives us happiness.

201.

We all know what's pleasurable, but happiness draws a blank.

202.

We all feel we know what's good for us, but that turns out to be our first mistake. Otherwise we would already be happy.

203.

We have so much desire to the exclusion of happiness that we don't know what happiness really is.

204.

Our mind has an amazing potential in that it will make us unhappy or happy by just depending on how we choose to use it.

205.

If we can see it doesn't get any better than life is now, we are happy.

206.

Everyone seems to feel they know how to make the best decisions, but if that were true everyone should be happy.

207.

Once we learn real happiness, life becomes much easier.

208.

Everyone knows what gives them pleasure, but few will ever know how to become happy.

209.

Happiness isn't pleasurable, but pleasure isn't happiness. While one feels good the other is good.

210.

Happiness is the promised land that will never happen. We can only get there by not listening to anyone else, not even ourselves.

211.
Pleasure is hard to acquire and maintain; happiness is easiest to have but hardest to find.

212.
We are never as sure of anything as much as when we are sure of the fact that we are happy now.

213.
People or our possessions will not make us happy because they can only give us pleasure.

214.
When we are not happy it is because we have not thought about it.

215.
Our minds will give us happiness when we learn to converse with ourselves.

216.
While we are being driven on for pleasure, we must become our driver of happiness.

217.
Our life's dedication to the pleasures of others instead of being alone in nature is happiness.

218.
When we stop running after all we desire, we may see life clearly and become happy.

219.
Peace and quiet is our greatest reward of happiness; the benefits of all our effort.

220.
If we don't think about what's meaningful we won't know what happiness is.

221.

Happiness is not pleasure; everyone may not know one is thinking while the other is emotions. One is to be trusted while the other is our demise in fun and excitement.

222.

We look out of ourselves for pleasure or within ourselves for happiness.

223.

The control of one's emotions, thus behavior is confidence in one's abilities to become happy over desires.

224.

All desire is temporary, while happiness is lasting.

225.

We can't run or we can't hide from ourselves any longer, for our happiness is at stake.

226.

We are not thinking or we would be happy now.

227.

Happiness is not fun or exciting because it is peaceful and calm.

228.

We all know what gives us pleasure, but now we must give ourselves happiness.

229.

To be happy, we have to know ourselves and life for a favorable opinion of both.

230.

We give to others what they want, or we give to ourselves what we need. We want pleasure, but we need happiness.

231.

Happiness is up to us because nobody else can give it to us.

232.

When we don't want pleasure anymore we will have found happiness: that's a choice only a few will ever know.

233.

We see life but we don't see ourselves clearly. If we did, we would be happy now.

234.

Happiness is a state of mind and not a fact of life.

235.

When we're not having fun or excitement, that's happiness; but we know it only as boring.

236.

We should relish time spent alone, instead we languish in time ill-spent because happiness is opposite of desire.

237.

Knowledge of others is for pleasure or knowledge of ourselves is for happiness.

238.

Perfection in our minds is not boring. It's an effect to become happy and not just fun or excitement, but peace and quiet instead.

239.

The best life we could have would be authority over us to be happy and not just pleasure or without much regard for what others feel was a success.

240.

If we had been thinking long ago we could have been happy all that time.

241.

When we have authority over ourselves wouldn't we want to be happy now? This would mean we could pre-determine our own future. The influence over our future we must pre-dispose now.

242.
We are controlled by pleasure or we are freed by happiness.

243.
Our lives are pleasure or happiness. We all make that choice: while one feels good the other is good.

244.
We may figure it out that a higher I.Q. won't make us happy. We can just have more pleasures.

245.
Loneliness is pleasure's enemy, but happiness's best friend,

246.
We must be kind to ourselves in order to become happy.

247.
Happiness is a true state of mind and not illusional or imaginary.

248.
We seem to be only as good as we think we are. So think good and be happy.

249.
We aren't thinking about life or we would already be happy now.

250.
Desire causes us to hurry up, but happiness causes us to slow down.

251.
We can't make anyone happy; they must do it for themselves.

252.
How can we ever feel we would be happy if we don't ever think?

253.
When we are happy it is because we know nothing else really matters.

254.
We are so very happy or so very sad, the choice is always ours to make.

255.
We are restricted by our desires, but we are liberated by our happiness.

256.
We must take risks to be happy.

257.
Intelligence will not afford us happiness.

258.
It is harder to get more than it is to let go and be happy.

259.
We seem to be running, scared, full of doubt, anxiety, fear for fear's sake. Not for our own happiness's sake.

260.
When we are the best we can become we can live with that happily.

261.
We are as happy or as unhappy as we think we are, that is our choice.

262.
We know what is up and what is down, yet we may not know what is sound or we would all be happy now.

263.
We don't need anyone to be happy, we only need others for pleasure.

264.
When we are happy we have got life figured out, while others are suffering.

265.
Transition from natural to function is how we must change ourselves in order to become happy. That is why nobody is happy.

266.

When we can't improve on our lives anymore we will know we are happy now.

267.

When we hold on so tight that we can't let go we can't know happiness as all risk has in it a reward or failure.

268.

When being with ourselves is not a burden then we are wise to be happy.

269.

We feel we know what is good; that is all we want. If so, why aren't we happy now?

270.

When we are not happy it's because we don't know how and never really wanted to.

271.

We long for lost pleasures, but happiness is timeless.

272.

Every decision we have made was probably wrong for us; if we are not happy now then we are doing something wrong.

273.

We can't become happy when we are so unhappy all the time, unless we know what happiness is not.

274.

We do what we want or what we need; therein lies the difference between pleasure and happiness.

275.

When we don't seek admiration we have all we need, when a simple life is all that we want and that is happiness.

276.

We're doing for pleasure or we're being for happiness.

277.

Either we know what to do to be quiet or we run around all the time. Which one of us is the happiest?

278.

Life is so good it is hard to believe we're really happy then all is as it should be.

279.

We all know enough to get by but not enough to become happy.

280.

When we are unhappy we must not know how to be happy now and forever.

281.

Happiness is related to pleasure, that if either is true or false the other is false or true.

282.

Freedom from fear is happiness. Full of fear is pain.

283.

We are all driven by what drives us. When we look inside ourselves, should life have been our pleasures or happiness?

284.

A life of senses doesn't make us happy.

285.

We deserve to be happy but we just don't know how.

286.

There isn't very much written about happiness. Maybe that is because they're so happy already. Why should they write?

287.

Pleasure or pain distracts from our well-being; by subtracting from our state of well-being isn't happy.

288.
Without doubt we know just what to do, yet we never know happiness.

289.
Our lives are happy when we have knowledge and influence over ourselves but not others for pleasures.

290.
When we limit our pleasures we'll find we are happier.

291.
Boredom is lost pleasures resisting happiness.

292.
All life is struggling between desire and fear, without happiness.

293.
We are happier when we have the least amount of desire.

294.
Our passive absorption in the contemplation of happiness is our rejection of desires.

295.
Our longevity depends on our happiness and not on how much pleasure we derived.

296.
Desire won't allow us to be happy.

297.
Value what we have and not just what is missing.

298.
Why do we always want what we do not have when we're not happy when we get it? For happiness is to become peaceful, calm, blissful, harmonious and heavenly.

299.
When we are happy, we are in charge of ourselves.

300.
Happiness is an informed choice.

301.
Happiness is a state of mind, but pleasure is outside of a state of mindfulness.

302.
Why do we do what we want to do instead of what we have to do to be happy?

303.
Our internal villain has an eternal design of desires that will stand between us and happiness.

304.
Our internal realization of being and not our external processes of doing give us the opportunity to know happiness.

305.
Everybody finds pleasure temporarily, but only a few know how to find permanent happiness.

306.
We must give up all thoughts of happiness for all our feelings of pleasure.

307.
Pleasure is not sustainable but happiness is.

308.
Contentment is just meaningful content that affects our happiness.

309.
We must give ourselves happiness while others give us pleasure.

310.
Happiness is the result of reason and logic, while pleasure is the result of basic motivations we would not fulfill if we thought about our lives.

311.
We want more but we really need less because more is for pleasure and less is for happiness.

312.
Unhappiness must not be ignored for it's a learning opportunity to know that desire isn't happiness and happiness isn't pleasure.

313.
To become happy we must learn what happiness does and does not do.

314.
That no one makes a conscious decision to be unhappy we know, but then all decisions don't result in happiness is a credibility gap between what we want and what we got.

315.
Maximal pleasure but minimal is happiness.

316.
We don't give up anything without finding something better. Our happiness is the gauge of our wisdom.

317.
It is our fault we are not happy.

318.
Our happiness must come from within our higher thinking alone, while desire for possessions and others' company is outside of our thinking.

319.
If we get what we sought and we are not happy, then we must not have sought happiness but some pleasures along the way.

320.
Regardless of what we may feel every day, the fact is it doesn't make us happy and goes unnoticed.

321.
Our clear thinking is its own reward that will go unnoticed without introspection. Our happiness is also a personal experience not to be shared with all who suffer.

322.
When we are free from our most controlling motives of pain or pleasure we have a favorable opportunity to become happy.

323.
It is not an equal chance for happiness as pleasure because so few are happy while everyone has pleasure to varying degrees.

324.
Just to be still within is our way to become peaceful and happy.

325.
While happiness is peace, our pleasure is folly. That is our two minds over our bodies.

326.
Just to be is an end destination itself. No place to go or nothing to do is our only peace and happiness.

327.
When we have more pleasure, we must feel we're going to be happy; but when we think about it, pleasure isn't happiness.

328.
Our happiness is the mind's ability to know life and itself for truth in our lifetimes.

329.
Peace from our ego, lust and fear is happiness from the endless desire for pleasure, resulting in fear of loss and life itself.

330.
We seem to have to suffer the loss of desire in order to gain happiness.

331.

What we do not know must be more important than what we do know if we are not happy now.

332.

We don't want to know how our minds work because all we want is fun and excitement. Well, that's how it works, but desire causes us stress, anxiety and turmoil. By not knowing how our minds work we're not happy.

333.

We do not deserve to be happy if we are not happy yet.

334.

Happiness is doing what you want to do and not what you have to do. Desire is doing what we have to do to get the pleasure you want.

335.

We are in a hurry for pleasure but must slow down for happiness.

336.

Happiness is not suffering the fear or loss of pleasure or the effort required to acquire pleasure all our lives.

337.

Let's consider what we have more of and what we want least. Wouldn't that make us happier?

338.

Pleasure is divine but happiness is sublime.

339.

We are governed by others for desire or we are governed by our higher thinking for happiness.

340.

Don't we affect ourselves or does life affect us? Know this to become happy.

341.
To know ourselves and to become happy from that experience is a success.

342.
We have to make the time because we won't find any to become happy.

343.
In nature is where we can receive a certain degree of happiness that resonates from within us.

344.
When we don't like ourselves, we cannot be happy.

345.
We are not wise because we are not happy! For a wise person is happy.

346.
Our ambitions are more stressful than any fame or fortune received and will never make us happy.

347.
If you're not happy, it is your fault. You selected pleasure instead.

348.
We are not happy because we don't know what happy really is.

349.
True happiness will come from our strengths and not from our weaknesses.

350.
It is troubling to be around others who are unhappy.

351.
Nature vs. society is happiness vs. desire.

352.
We are the only ones that can bring us happiness.

353.
Do you want to be happy now or maybe tomorrow?

354.
Unhappiness is dysfunctional thinking.

355.
Freedom is controlling what controls us. Then peace from us is happiness now.

356.
When we are not happy it is our fault.

357.
Happiness is realized in the moments of our day and not in the goals we attain.

358.
We are never going to become happy with others.

359.
Now is our time to live yet we are still unhappy because that is the only thing missing.

360.
Maybe we are not happy because we don't know how to be.

361.
Happiness is our gift to ourselves.

362.
The finest thing in life turns out to be life itself.

363.
We could make time to be happy but we don't think how.

364.
Happiness is being alive and knowing what life really means.

365.
Pleasures are temporarily attainable on various levels, but happiness is harder to know and much less accessible.

366.
To become as peaceful as nature is happiness.

367.
We must like ourselves in order to become happy.

368.
To postpone happiness is to postpone our life because tomorrow never comes.

369.
Maybe we're the problem is why we're not happy now.

370.
Stress limits our ability to make long term decisions, so we focus on today's problems and not on solutions for tomorrow without any consideration of happiness.

371.
Good is happy, bad is unhappy.

372.
Our happiness is a state of mind we have to know and compel ourselves to do. It's good to be happy, and happy by choice.

373.
Our happiness is without any desires or fears.

374.
Don't do any injustices to ourselves or others if we want to be happy; but if we do, learn by our mistakes.

375.
We aren't happy because we don't have a clue, otherwise everyone would be happy too.

376.
To become happy we must have governed ourselves to become right.

377.
What we want is not what we need to become happy.

378.
We desire pleasure, but we don't desire happiness, otherwise we would be happy now.

379.
Why not stop what we've been doing all our lives if we're not happy from doing it?

380.
We must not desire to know what happiness is, because it doesn't give us pleasure.

381.
Without doubt we are defenseless.

382.
Without desire there is no pleasure.

383.
Without pleasure there is happiness.

384.
We seek pleasure in all that we do, but happiness is found in the stillness of being.

385.
Happiness is in not desiring anything.

386.
Emotions make us slaves to our senses, while thinking makes us free to be happy.

387.
Pleasure may be harmful. Happiness is helpful.

388.

When we can't think of how to improve on our lives we are content.

389.

Intellect may subtract from our happiness.

390.

Happiness isn't what everyone is seeking otherwise they would have found it by now.

391.

Technology and globalization gives us pleasure, but not happiness.

392.

When we follow the least path of resistance we will be happy all the way. We will have the most to be happy for if we don't look away from that possibility.

393.

It is much easier to be a good person than it is to be a bad person, when what rules our lives is happiness and not pleasure.

394.

We travel to have pleasure, we buy to have pleasure and we work to have pleasure, but without pleasure we would be free to be happy.

395.

We have held on to all that promises to be pleasurable and found it easier to let go of anything that might promise us happiness.

396.

We may be alone, broke, tired and unhappy or we may be alone, broke, tired and happy, for happiness is a state of mind.

397.

Pleasure can be seen, heard, tasted, smelled and felt, but happiness can't be seen, heard, tasted, smelled or felt. This is why we have trouble knowing happiness is in our minds and much more subtle than emotions.

398.
All others will follow anyone who might promise pleasure, but nobody will follow those who might promise happiness because it's not fun or exciting.

399.
When we no longer require ownership or companionship we will have acquired contentment and happiness.

400.
We may be the cause of our own unhappiness without knowing what happiness is supposed to do.

401.
This could be the best day of our lives, but without us knowing happiness it's just another day.

402.
Those who realize they are not happy are beginning a long journey now.

CHAPTER NINETEEN

ENLIGHTENMENT:
Our wisdom back upon our minds function

1.
Enlightenment is the result of turning our wisdom back upon our mind's functions and from that knowledge we can become the cause of the effects of our life.

2.
Enlightenment is leaving everything we most loved behind.

3.
The window to our enlightenment is narrow, but there is an opening. The journey to our enlightenment is arduous otherwise we would not have ventured.

4.
This is an internal voyage into our two minds to know and be known like a worm hole into our inner space. When we emerge again we will never be the same.

5.
Ignorance doesn't know intelligence, intelligence doesn't know wisdom, wisdom doesn't know enlightenment; but enlightenment must know all three.

6.
Enlightenment is a flickering candle in the darkness of our minds.

7.
There is a window into our minds, but it is hard to find. When we don't look it is closed all the time.

8.
Self-induced poverty is our enlightenment over the bondage of desires and fears.

9.
We desire for more, but wisdom must question and enlightenment does neither.

10.
When our willfulness equals our stillness then we are static.

11.
The highest mental achievement would be enlightenment yet no one says they want to be enlightened.

12.
When we're enlightened we don't want to change anything anymore.

13.
Wisdom is our mind's influence over our senses, while all enlightenment is just the stillness of our mind over itself.

14.
When we awaken, we all can see the affects we have had upon our lives without us thinking. Awakening of this inward state of the outward facts is enlightening.

15.
Our enlightenment is the result of our willingness to slay the dragon within.

16.
Enlightenment is an inward state of an outward fact that is not dulled by our mind.

17.
Life will kill all the messengers-one and all-for they are not important anymore. The message they found is all that will last.

18.
Enlightenment is living the dream but not the fantasy.

19.
We all know what it is to be human, but what would life be like if we were an enlightened human?

20.
We are like a stranger within ourselves for there is another mind that is all knowing and very quiet.

21.
What is the purpose of life? Life is the purpose of life!

22.
We must turn our mind back upon itself in order to stop us from thinking outside of ourselves, to know the source of our enlightenment.

23.
When turning the light of reason upon ourselves we will become enlightened.

24.
Enlightenment is to progress to a point of competence.

25.
We must focus on the distance traveled toward enlightenment and not on the pleasures lost along the way. This is our greatest accomplishment of life.

26.
When we don't want to do anything, time seems to stop in the present moment. Now I won is time and place I dwell and abide.

27.
Loneliness is a barrier to entry to enlightenment; nobody gets there because it is not fun or exciting, but peaceful and calm.

28.
Wisdom is doing what we need to do and not what we want to do. Then enlightenment is not doing anything at all.

29.
We don't have to go to the ends of the earth to find ourselves, for enlightenment is the light we find in our minds and the silence of the ages.

30.
If enlightenment is from our desires for pleasure or fear and pain then everyone would be enlightened now.

31.
Life's quest has taken us all over until we become our own conquest. The journey of searching is over when we find ourselves.

32.
Enlightenment is a journey. The higher one gets the farther we can see. We must still go.

33.
We think and we think and we think we know. Maybe we don't think and maybe we don't know. We could turn the light back onto ourselves to become enlightened.

34.
There is a vast untouched base of enlightenment in all of us, but we must look inward to find it.

35.
Life is so sweet when we rule ourselves out.

36.
Enlightenment derives knowledge, peace and happiness by withdrawal from society.

37.
We would not know if a person is enlightened, we would have to be told.

38.
When we think about enlightenment that's the first step of an endless journey.

39.
Within us there is another all-knowing separate self, hidden but aware of us and life.

40.
Enlightened heads for a target that no one else can see.

41.
Enlightenment is an endless journey that can only be measured in the distance we've traveled.

42.
Enlightenment is all-knowing, we can never know.

43.
Enlighten is anytime we manage to beat back the darkness in our mind.

44.
We must turn the searchlight back upon ourselves to find out that nothing is missing.

45.
Our efforts may not be worth the rewards if we never know ourselves for true meaning.

46.
When we are always looking outside of ourselves for answers, we never look inside for the questions.

47.
A visionary conceives ideas and projects not regarded by others.

48.
Influence over ourselves is blocked by clouds of desires and fear so we can't see a way for the light is outside of us. When the light is in us, the way becomes clear.

49.
Everything points to the way, except we must learn to know ourselves for we are our hindrance, otherwise everyone would be enlightened.

50.
To look inside one's own mind for its contents is to turn inward to know oneself, so as to become enlightened.

51.
If a wise person knows timing, then an enlightened person knows themself.

52.
Once we acquire wisdom it is very hard to go back to our old ways. That didn't work very well anyway. When we see clearly we can see much farther inside.

53.
It is what we don't know that turns out to be the most important.

54.
It is gratifying to know the importance of life's impermanence as we age.

55.
There is greatness within our mind that we must seek before we can find.

56.
Our attachment causes suffering, but to know un-attachment is our contentment.

57.
Our lower mind must gain a reverence for our higher thinking in order to see life clearly so as to become one with our self.

58.
Earthism is the belief that this earth is the best possible place for our happiness.

59.
Enlightenment is to become at peace with life and ourselves.

60.
An enlightened person must become like a grain of sand on the beach.

61.
Our minds are like a coin in that each side is looking in the opposite direction, but both sides occupy the same body.

62.
Our quality of life is inversely proportionate to our standard of living. That's just the opposite of what everyone feels and seeks.

63.
Life's not for the brass ring, it is for the ride.

64.
All anyone really has is time, but all we do is waste it.

65.
Enlightenment is obstructed by all the clouds in our minds. We can only know this when the clouds are fewer.

66.
If you've found all you're looking for, then you've found yourself.

67.
Enlightenment is like a full moon over a dark night.

68.
It takes an entire lifetime to find ourselves and that's if we are looking.

69.
Stillness of our self brings enlightenment.

70.
Our lives unfold from within us.

71.

Life tests us all, but it is up to us to test ourselves. Self-evident truths and common sense are the best two friends we will ever have.

72.

If we're not living our dream then we either don't know how to dream or live so life's just a job.

73.

To understand our mind is to understand our lives.

74.

We are king or queen of our castles, but few are king or queen of themselves.

75.

When there is no place to go or we have nothing to do then our upper mind has made us free from ourselves.

76.

This world is the best possible world, but only realized by our highest state of mind.

77.

The third way is enlightenment.

78.

To really appreciate every day is not looking ahead to tomorrow or back to yesterday.

79.

The hardest things to know are: what we do not know is why we do not know.

80.

A state of being and not just doing is the ultimate nature of our minds as opposed to our existence for our demands.

81.

Our best outlook turns out to be in-look. (In ourselves.)

82.
The greatest accomplishment in life is in understanding our own minds.

83.
Death is life's infinity of nothingness.

84.
When we open our mind up we will let the light in.

85.
Enlightenment is self-evident.

86.
When we are above it all then we are doing it right.

87.
Our greatest discovery will have been our minds.

88.
Enlightenment is above wisdom and without pleasure.

89.
Wisdom is what is done, but enlightenment is what is not done.

90.
When we do not care we are there.

91.
Maybe we lost much more than we spent on all those possessions we hold so dear, for they did take a lifetime you know.

92.
Enlightenment was in the sights of our vision.

93.
Higher thinking, wisdom and enlightenment are hard to do because they are not fun or exciting.

94.
Pleasure comes from others while happiness comes from within, so does wisdom and enlightenment.

95.
When our frontal lobes are facing in the true direction of our life we have our head on right; it is from the top down and not from the bottom up.

96.
We don't know where we are going when we haven't been there yet.

97.
We are the light into ourselves or not.

98.
To know the unknown is just to know ourselves.

99.
We can become a sanctuary from ourselves and life.

100.
Arise to the moment or lose it all together.

101.
Our greatest good is a communion of our mind with itself.

102.
We have more mental potential available than the willingness to acquire its use.

103.
An enlightened person does not want anyone to know they are enlightened.

104.
We follow our light or live in darkness.

105.
The unknown elephant in our room turns out to be the mind.

106.
We must know ourselves in order to be our masters.

107.
We may run all our lives without ever knowing ourselves because that was never a question.

108.
Enlightenment could come after our darkness, but we must shed the old to have the new.

109.
All life's an opportunity and not a problem so we should stop always looking for problems in order to see life's opportunities.

110.
We must just want to be entertained and not to be enlightened.

111.
There is a window into our minds but it is hard to find.

112.
Enlightenment don't go, stay a little longer.

113.
If we could see our future we would not do what we are doing right now.

114.
The planning of our lives shouldn't extend past the day.

115.
Life doesn't get any better when we figure it out. We've only got a lifetime so we had better be right.

116.
To know the unknown is an ability to know ourselves.

117.
Our mind is like a toy, we can play with it or observe its workings.

118.
Make mindful every mile for life is just a little while.

119.
The only way to become liberated is through ourselves.

120.
To be conscious of consciousness is to turn our light back upon ourselves and become enlightened.

121.
Insight into ourselves is enlightening.

122.
Our mind has a mind of its own.

123.
A god free life is a carefree life.

124.
Enlightenment doesn't fight or flee.

125.
The greatest light is the light we shine on ourselves.

126.
We can't add anything to life without detracting from life itself.

127.
Our life's experiences are either stifling or enlightening, but that choice just happens to be ours.

128.
Enlightened is a win for happiness but a loss for pleasure.

129.
An enlightened person knows what to do by doing nothing.

130.
Enlightenment is the knowledge, intelligence and will over ourselves.

131.
An examination of our thought processes is toward an axis of growth.

132.
To know the minds of many others is not worth the time of not knowing just one percent of our own mind.

133.
Our greatness is in the ability to overcome our mind's limitations by exercising the scope of its influence over itself.

134.
When we seek light, we will find it within us by knowing this.

135.
Looking at life for most is like us looking through a key hole. We become so intent to see as much as we can, we never see ourselves.

136.
The harmonious arrangement of the order of our minds would have to be considered before it could be realized.

137.
Life's greatest reward turns out to also be life's greatest secret. We have a mind but we desire not to use it.

138.
We seem to want to know of all things except ourselves. For life's greatest secret is ourselves.

139.
Enlightenment is the ability to see life clearly in order to be wise in life's decisions.

140.
The greatest story never told is the unknown enlightenment of our higher thinking.

141.
Enlightenment is the result of examining one's own mind though processes and not the emotional systems interruption of that process.

142.
Enlightening is a blessing, but becomes a burden when we live alone. When we're enlightened, it is too late to go back.

143.
It is enlightening to know nothing needs to be done.

144.
Let us see how far we can go, but first we must start with ourselves.

145.
If a troubled mind is to be the human condition, then an untroubled mind is to become enlightened.

146.
We can't give up yet just because we haven't gotten there yet, or we may never know our highest purpose of life was to just know ourselves.

147.
There is an eternal quality of our mental capacity to determine our best course of actions.

148.
Our mind will explode with delight when we finally see the light, as all minds will see the dawn of their own insights.

149.
Our enlightenment is to be found within our own inner space.

150.
We are just like puppets in the scheme of life when we don't know the puppeteer could be us.

151.
Life is so enlightening when we look into ourselves. We are the cause of tomorrow so had better figure it out now and not tomorrow. (Sooner is better.)

152.
There is only now and that's everything.

153.
To know the moment above all else is golden.

154.
It is not where we are that's as important as where our minds are now.

155.
No reasons to think or do but to just be is all there really is anyways.

156.
When we find what we seek it will have been ourselves.

157.
Life is great and we have it now.

158.
To seek happiness over desire or fear is enlightenment.

159.
Lust in the dust. Past in the trash. Run is not fun. Quest for a rest.

160.
We've won when we learned the battle was within us.

161.
There can be greatness found in us all, but we have to be looking.

162.
Our greatest accomplishment is just authority over ourselves.

163.
The most important opinion is what we have of ourselves.

164.
We will be gone very soon so how important is now?

165.
We have to give up everything in order to know ourselves.

166.
When our will leaves us, we can see this life is a very special place.

167.
The greatest good is the knowledge our mind has of itself.

168.
When we know enough about our self, then we can't be controlled anymore. We are free.

169.
While we are obsessing over our life's details, we are missing the wonders of life itself.

170.
Enlightenment is self-awareness so as to live a deliberate life without desires or fears.

171.
One who is enlightened has a pleasurable life, but is free to leave.

172.
An unexamined life is an uninformed life.

173.
We must shine light onto the darkness of our minds.

174.
When we will ourselves by our mental facilities we are self-realized.

175.
Our greatest growth is to focus inward in order to eliminate our limitations.

176.
The height of obsession is not to be obsessed anymore.

177.
We can escape ourselves imposed bounds that bind us all.

178.
There is so much to consider and so little time to consider.

179.
Our greatness comes from within our minds and not from others.

180.
It is lonely when we try to fly higher than anyone else.

181.
This is the greatest moment of our lives, but without that knowledge it is just another day.

182.
There is a voice within us that is hard to hear.

183.
Enlightenment is all around us and shines on the darkness of our minds, but is unknown.

184.
Our greatest good is the knowledge we can acquire of ourselves.

185.
The winds of time will make dust of our bones, so how important are our lives now?

186.
Those who restrict their ego, lust and fear will know what no one else will.

187.
We are the difference between an average life and a wonder-filled life.

188.
When we're finally free, we have learned how to be free from ourselves.

189.
A synopsis of our synapsis is introspection, like a mirror of our minds.

190.
Our greatness is beyond a vision when it is even beyond a request.

191.
What a delight to commune with our mind.

192.
Self-law are rules we created by reason on our behalf.

193.
We are currently living a life we can't escape from or we are living a life we escaped from. We escape from ourselves or not.

194.
To become aware of a higher order of our minds is blissful.

195.
When we know what we need then there is less room for what we want.

196.
The real prize was in our minds, but our focus is on what we see.

197.
Our life is everything because without that there is nothing.

198.
Let there be light and that light must come from within us as the cause of all our tomorrows.

199.
Enlightenment travels from left to right.

200.
It is not the messenger but the message that's meaningful or not.

201.
Our lives are a privilege, but unrealized.

202.
It is a lonely life when we are informed because no one else seems to know the way.

203.
There is a part of our mind that is unknown to us that's peaceful all the time.

204.
To become insightful is apprehension of the inner nature of our self.

205.
Our mind is the cause of the rest of our life. There can't be anything as important as the quality of our mind.

206.
Life is not where we are going but where we are now.

207.
To write for light is self-discovery.

208.
We must be fearless for our minds ability to better ourselves.

209.
We may not know what we have in us because we never look.

210.
Enlightened is to see life clearly and ourselves profoundly.

211.
There is greatness in all our minds; we need only to look within and not outside of us.

212.
The best company is our self without us knowing.

213.
We must open our minds to let the light come in.

214.
To know the unknown is to know ourselves, so we must let go in order to see ourselves more clearly.

215.
There is a greater self if we would only listen.

216.
We will change our world if we can change ourselves.

217.
We all come and then we must go, but the time spent in between is all we will ever know. So how important is life?

218.
Only the curious will discover themselves.

219.
By taming the beast within we are freed from ourselves.

220.
Our greatest victory would have been over ourselves.

221.
We are the problem when we are not the solution. Does enlightenment come from within us?

222.
There is greatness in our minds when we approach an awareness of thinking clearly, let the light shine in.

223.
Our greatness must come from within and not from any other.

224.
A prophet doesn't derive profits from others.

225.
All goodness is success over ourselves.

226.
We can't seem to control ourselves without knowing ourselves.

227.
Our mind must become a higher state in order to live in a higher state of life.

228.
Reality is an escape from ourselves.

229.
To know our self is to finally be right.

230.
How far we go means we have to look up.

231.
We must know ourselves in order to be whole.

232.
All of our enlightenment comes from within us.

233.
If we haven't risked then we haven't gained. Take all the risk we can because we'll learn more when risk has no gain.

234.
What a great life it is when we're in tune with ourselves.

235.
There is something in having nothing that makes us understand what's really important was life.

236.

Our truth to our self will make our lives ours. For all we will ever have is our self. Everything alive is temporary.

237.

Life is greater when we can become the self-made cause of our motivations.

238.

We must slow ourselves down in order to know what we're missing.

239.

We get the most out of no.

240.

When we are always out there, we are never in here.

241.

Our feelings are on possessions or others, either past or future. When our mind is on now, we are free from what controls us, which is us.

242.

Perfection is to be alive and know what life means.

243.

Time is our friend not our enemy.

244.

The best life we can lead is to know ourselves, and in that knowledge we will have deserved our respect.

245.

We will know when we're at our best, the reward is we will like our self; that's as good as it can get.

246.

Life is everything because without that we have nothingness.

247.

The only trouble for us was the trouble we cause ourselves.

248.
We would have to become introspective to know ourselves, so as to bring us into compliance in order to value life to its highest degree.

249.
Life does not get any better than it is but we can.

250.
We are just the observers of life because life doesn't observe us.

251.
We only have ourselves until the end.

252.
We see what we want, but we don't see what we have.

253.
The message is what's meaningful and not the messenger.

254.
When we are controlled the most we are least ourselves.

255.
The bigger our dreams, the greater our endeavors.

256.
When we consider the possibilities we have taken the first step of our life's journey.

257.
When we are happy, we don't need much; but when we're the happiest, we don't want anything.

258.
We must give of ourselves to have a full life experience.

259.
We can become an amusement to ourselves.

260.
Life is too good for us when we know this.

261.
What better way to know ourselves than to write our thoughts on paper?

262.
To mine our mind is introspection.

263.
Life is awe-filled, but we seem to make it awful.

264.
To become all we can be is really everything we are. Nothing is more important than our lives when we know this.

265.
We must write before we think to be uninhibited.

266.
When we let go, we have caught on; once we have caught on, we can't let go.

267.
We want of all things except of ourselves.

268.
When we want to stop in our tracks and go no further, we are free from ourselves.

269.
Our lives are made more meaningful by what we have given up than what we could ever acquire.

270.
There is greatness within us when we take time to know ourselves.

271.
Our time is worth more than all the fame and fortune in the world.

272.
Life is simple but is so hard to figure out.

273.
Our highest state of mind is the culmination of perception, realization and knowledge.

274.
When all we are is a good person, isn't that really everything?

275.
The most informed would not give up everything without receiving something even better.

276.
Accept life as it is and not as we want it to be, but accept ourselves as we want to be and not as we are now.

277.
Our lives can evolve to or from a higher form of ourselves.

278.
We are compelled or we compel.

279.
The pre-determination of any life is the existence of life itself. It is everything for everybody.

280.
We're captured by our weaknesses or we're liberated by our strengths.

281.
We own our lives or our lives own us. That's the difference between being a master or slave of ourselves.

282.
We are more entertaining than others or possessions.

283.
Our life's decisions are pre-determined by ancient instinctive emotions instead of our current higher state of reasoning.

284.
We are really all we've got.

285.
In order to think clearly, we have to stop feeling good.

286.
Enlightenment knows the cause and effects, but does neither and becomes the doer and not the done.

287.
Enlightenment decreases our suffering from self-inflicting desires and fears.

288.
An enlightened person is peaceful with all of life, and themselves.

289.
There's a fine line between wisdom and enlightenment, but a real life in the differences.

290.
These are my three steps to enlightenment: philosophy, wisdom, and neuropathic systems knowledge.

291.
If wisdom knows timing then enlightenment knows restraint in all things.

292.
Enlightenment is the ultimate nature of being and not just existence.

293.
Be enlightened or go home.

294.
Pleasure screams, happiness talks, enlightenment just whispers.

295.
The greatest distance traveled in life is from the mind of a child's to enlightenment.

296.
When our goal in life is to become enlightened we are on our way.

297.
That enlightenment is not fun or exciting is why I see so few along the way who are enlightened.

298.
I may not be enlightened, but there is no one I've known who was to say.

299.
Our greatest discovery is ourselves.

300.
Time rests in the stillness of our minds.

301.
When we're indifferent good or bad doesn't pertain to us much anymore.

302.
It would take days of quietness to find true quietness and that's if we were trying.

303.
In the stillness of our minds we'll find wisdom, empathy, consciousness, awareness, apathy, higher thinking, and enlightenment.

304.
Enlightenment is our highest calling with the fewest applicants.

305.
There is very little known of wisdom or enlightenment, so progress will be easy for the few who dare to tread for their highest calling.

306.
When life is enough we have all the time for ourselves.

307.
Anyone or anything we choose to follow will surely take us away from enlightenment.

308.
There is greatness in our minds if we take the time to find the unseen is insight, the unknown is knowledge, the light is enlightenment.

309.
Our greatness is not what we have, where we've been, or who we are, but what's within the stillness of our minds.

310.
We will develop smugness from our foolishness or wisdom, but not from our enlightenment.

311.
All youth knows what's important but old age knows what's unimportant.

312.
We seem to have to compete for all things in our lives, except enlightenment is without much competition.

313.
Maybe our greatest accomplishment is just to have known and respected ourselves as the benefactor of all life's experiences.

314.
We can acknowledge life's appearances but the profound seems at first unfathomable.

315.
The outer world seems to offer confusion while the inner world seems to offer order.

316.
When the stillness of the early morning matches the stillness of our minds we are being and not doing.

317.
Enlightenment is like looking through a two way mirror.

CHAPTER TWENTY

HEAVEN:
We are in heaven now

1.
If we are the highest consciousness on earth, that should afford us the ability to comprehend the highest realization. That is we are in heaven now, if we think about it.

2.
Heaven now isn't a religious belief, it's a process of consciousness, the realization of life's value is to have lived and to know this.

3.
Impermanence is all life's course, without fear that knowledge is acceptance of life as it is and not as we want it to be.

4.
We are so lucky to be alive and happy when we know we're in heaven, there is no waiting to die.

5.
We need to know where we are at now before we can say where we are going after our death.

6.
Heaven is now and not in some imaginary life after death, that is the effects of our desires and fears.

7.
Nature is the essence of life, a constant force that can be seen as heaven now on earth.

8.
The ultimate gratitude we can experience is that we know we are in heaven now.

9.
I can't be any happier than I am now. Alone but not lonely, without money but not poor, nothing to do and no place to go, but heaven is all about me, this I know.

10.
What goals would we have if we knew we were in heaven on earth now?

11.
It is so peaceful and quiet early in the morning. The sun is just coming up and can hardly wait for another wonderful day in heaven all alone, so peaceful and quiet.

12.
Life is a wondrous place of utmost harmony and order when we understand heaven is now in this place.

13.
Happiness is doing less and being happier. We didn't expect to do anything much in heaven. Well, we are in heaven now.

14.
The difference between an ordinary life and an exceptional life is to know you are in heaven.

15.
We are feeling and not thinking to feel; we would have to die to be reborn again so as to be in heaven when all we have to do is to think now.

16.
When we are happy, we start to think we're in heaven now. Isn't that the best life we could make for ourselves?

17.
When we don't think we are in heaven now, that's a day we don't know life in a very special way.

18.
Our opportunity of the moment is knowing that we are in heaven now. In this way, we gain by turning life into our best advantage.

19.
Heaven could be a doctrine that this world is the best possible world if we choose the life we live as the most favorable condition for happiness.

20.
We will most likely lose our lives before we acknowledge how wonderful life was.

21.
When anything dies it has been taken out of heaven by the laws of nature for heaven's sake.

22.
When we think we are in heaven now, our lives will become meaningful because where our minds go we do too.

23.
We are on a natural course of self-destruction without knowing we could become in harmony with life and ourselves to know we are in heaven now.

24.
When we think we will know we are in heaven now life will take on a new brilliance by embracing life's best and rejecting the worst.

25.
People come and people go but few ever know where they were at in life. Think on this and you will know all about heaven.

26.
The two of us are in heaven right now and that makes one of us very happy.

27.
We are so close to heaven but so far from knowing it.

28.
When we know we're in heaven now, we'll know more than anyone else seems to know.

29.
When our upper mind is thinking we are in heaven on earth now, that is to see life clearly free from ourselves.

30.
Death is our last day in heaven then we are off to hell, the absence of life.

31.
When we think heaven is now, then heaven is now.

32.
When we know we're in heaven nothing will detract from this moment except us.

33.
No one knows they are in heaven because they have never thought about it. When we know this nothing else really matters.

34.
A lonely life has its own rewards: it is peaceful, calm, tranquil, quiet, blissful and harmonious. Heaven is just to become happy.

35.
When we can say our lives can never get any better than it is now, then we are in heaven.

36.
If we don't think we are in heaven, then we are not thinking at all.

37.
When our choice doesn't seem like it would be in heaven, then do not choose it.

38.
We won't feel we're in heaven now. We have to think about it instead.

39.
When we don't know how this is heaven then life is just a job.

40.
We're so concerned about where we are going, we haven't thought about where we are at now.

41.
Our perception of heaven is facing inward toward our axis of growth.

42.
When we don't think it can get any better, then we know we're in heaven.

43.
We are spoiling heaven on earth and the canary in the mine.

44.
Heaven is in all that we see or do without us knowing.

45.
We make nothing in life; all we do is assemble the pieces. In fact we can't even make a weed.

46.
Yesterday is in all that we see or do without us knowing.

47.
Jesus and Buddha's true teachings were lost because they did not write the book themselves.

48.
It is far more important to know where we are now than where we feel we could go after we are dead.

49.
We are the beginning and ending of our life, and all in between was heaven.

50.
When we think we are in heaven now, we can't think any better.

51.
When we know we are in heaven now we are happy and we don't want anything else.

52.
We'll have a heavenly moment when we realize where we are.

53.
To become governed by our higher thinking is heaven on earth.

54.
We should take time to stand still when life doesn't get any better than it is. We are in heaven because we know it.

55.
Heaven, we're literally standing in it right now but don't know it.

56.
We may feel we know where we are going at death. What we don't think is where we are at now.

57.
Now I won true freedom that's peaceful, calm, tranquil, blissful and harmonious. Our happiness is heaven on earth right now.

58.
If we are not in heaven then we must feel we're in hell. All of our own making, couldn't we tell?

59.
Know this! Now is heaven.

60.
Life is such a grind everyday by our making. We cannot see we are within heaven's gates all the time without our awakening.

61.
Heaven is life now, and hell is the absence of life forever.

62.
We are in our heaven or hell of our own making. One is happiness the other is desire.

63.
When our lives are in heaven now we have realized this time and place.

64.
Our lives are spent in heaven on earth without knowing the importance of every moment.

65.
The gates of heaven on earth are within our minds for we all cause stress and anxiety or peace and calm.

66.
Paradise is in the knowing and not in the doing.

67.
Life is in heaven now but we don't think about it.

68.
Real opportunity is this moment in heaven now.

69.
Heaven is our life without a dopamine drip bag of desires.

70.
Heaven or hell is in the minds of everyone's choices as based on ignorance, foolishness or wisdom.

71.
All that we experience is either good, bad, or indifferent in heaven, except for our knowing.

72.
If we knew these were our last days we would want to be peaceful, calm, and tranquil.

73.
Life is so wonderful but why can we not know this?

74.
Heaven is what to see in all life.

75.
This is heaven, so be happy in that knowledge of our life.

76.
Life is so good we just don't have the time to know where we are now; we have to be our own driver in order to see ourselves clearly.

77.
To be wise beyond our years is to know we are in heaven now.

78.
Becoming free from the instincts that govern us all without our knowledge, influence or will is to be in heaven now.

79.
Life is heaven if we realize it, but it is like hell if we don't.

80.
Lakes, rivers and oceans know me very well.

81.
We don't have to die to go to heaven.

82.
We are in heaven except for our knowing, but when we do know this life becomes self-evident. Time and place I dwell and abide.

83.
Alive is heaven and death is hell.

84.
Higher thinking is heaven on earth, but our motivations are disturbing on earth.

85.
We are either living the fantasy of desires and fears, or the dream of heaven on earth as determined by emotions or reasons.

86.
Heaven on earth now is a religion of life, for life.

87.
All of life is in heaven now, but without enlightenment to know it.

88.
All life is in heaven and paradise is what we can make of it.

89.
We know the beginning of our lives and will know the ending of our lives, but the present is in heaven and without knowing.

CHAPTER TWENTY-ONE

PROFOUND CONCLUSION:
Pleasure is meaningless and happiness is meaningful

Nature created the human species and has given us our instinctual motivation for survival. Then from the randomness of nature's processes was developed a mutation of our higher thinking (cerebral cortex). This addition for planning is the state of a conscious mental process that has been very successful for our advancement to the top of the food chain. That in this success also lays our ability to destroy this life as we know it. Our original motivations of a desire for pleasure and fear of pain is resulting in damaging our environment, over population, ability for mass destruction and reducing our quality of life. Our need to realize this is by utilizing our higher thinking abilities of knowledge, influence, and will to supersede our instinctive motivations. After all, nature's original design models did self-destruct, for extinction in life has been successful over 98% of the time.

What we do not know seems to be more important than what we do know as a species. That would be why we: Eat too much of the wrong foods, commit crimes against society, drug abuse, cause harm to our environment, government abuse of authority, corporate power to control society, warring societies, causing danger to ourselves in risky activities, one gun per person, more murders per capita than any other country, viewing so much death and destruction on camera, risky sexual activities, compulsive gambling, religious intolerance, spending more hours working, spending more money than we make individually and as a nation, crime is rampant, moral decay of our society, bulging penal system, violence, not caring for our health. This is all done without a clear understanding that the cause of our dysfunctional society is a reflection of those individuals within that make it up.

The cause of all of our problems listed is basic to one common denominator, which are the natural instinctive motivations in all of us, quite simply: "A desire for pleasure and fear of pain." This is not unknown to everyone, but unrealized as our core motivations because we do not think when it comes to the fun and excitement of pleasure and resent anyone or anything including ourselves from threatening to diminish any self-destructive desire. We cannot get enough of what we do not need. Just try to limit our pleasure of the senses that is predisposing us, but also harmful to us in the end.

As an adult we use our mind's higher thinking for memory and planning, even our intelligence is for the maximum success of our lowest motivation that is without reason or logic. Our lives are the effects of causes we never question from birth till death, but are simply what instinctually nature demands of us. These are meaningless decisions for pleasure that are just temporary and must be reinforced over again and again. We are controlled in the most effective way possible because we do not feel we are being controlled; but feeling is not thinking.

When we feel the most free is when we are free to choose any desire we can have. We do not know we are not free because we do not desire to be free or it would give us less pleasure, when the greatest success in our society is anyone who has the most toys from fame or fortune. Why should the smartest people of our society use those greater capacities to make more money for fun and excitement? Instead of using that potential mental awareness to become conscious of themselves and direct their lives to what was meaningful, and away from what was meaningless so as to become happy all the days of their lives? In a society we give pleasure to others in hopes of receiving pleasure in return: it's a barter system of emotions.

In history some individuals or segments of societies have purposely isolated themselves from others so as to reduce or even eliminate their "Desire for pleasure or fear of pain." Although this is an extreme lifestyle change for anyone to consider, the utopias never seem to have been successful for very long. This needs to be an individual decision to be conscious of our weaknesses and strengths so as to direct ourselves for a deliberate life by our strengths and not our weaknesses. When this is successful we will almost eliminate all our stress, anxiety and despair (S.A.D.). This interferes with our highest thinking that's for peace, calm, tranquility, bliss and harmony, and our happiness instead of pleasure.

Isn't all money a desire for pleasure, fear of pain, and religion and politics, too? They are our feeling of emotions and not our higher thinking. All the struggles of the human race seem to be within ourselves between pleasure of our senses and happiness in our higher thinking. Until we know this and have influence over ourselves, we will always be living in the effects and not the cause of our lives. To successfully be able to regulate our lives from emotions to thinking. This can be accomplished by conscious planning and deliberation of our future by reducing a desire for pleasure or fear of pain that are basic instinctual responses. This instinctual demand of our neuropathic system of reward and punishment through our emotions is a value system controlled by a nonconscious process. That is the need for us to self-direct a conscious control process of our higher thinking for an awareness of our true motives. These nonconscious controls "If it feels good we want to do it" are biological biases that make us feel we are in control when we are just not thinking. This is why we are conflicted in all of our life's decisions from what feels good and what is good, which is desire vs. wisdom.

Our appetite system has been controlling us all our lives without us knowing why we are having the resulting problems we have now. Suffering, pain, and fear of loss is the negative feedback for a possible learning opportunity, but never seems to even alter our basic motivations. The constraint of a nonconscious automatic response of stimuli is unmeasurable because that's all we know. That if anything looks, smells, tastes, feels, or sounds desirable we want that pleasure. This is not thinking, but will result in a life of stress, anxiety and despair (S.A.D.) with a short-lived pleasure in return. We may know what we desire from birth till death, but our emotions are the same as a child's, by using our basic feelings only to the extent of fulfilling our instinctual motivations. All of life seems to be in living like a puppet whose acts are controlled by forces out of our control. When we become the puppeteer by use of our higher thinking, we avoid any problems associated with desire or fear that's a sweet fantasy and also a nightmare, too. Our higher thinking could become a reasonable cause of the effects of our lives and not nature's demands.

Enlightenment is just the result of turning our higher thinking back upon our own mind's functions, and from that knowledge we could become the cause of the effects of our life. The reward of this higher thinking is happiness and to that degree we will also become enlightened. The interest and curiosity that leads to inquiry into one's own mind for its contents by examination of both thought processes and sensory responses is indispensable in the effort to know and direct ourselves. This introspection into ourselves for the true cause of our lives is to actually know what is meaningless or meaningful. When we acquire the knowledge of how our mind functions and influences us in order to know what to do at any given time is our wisdom. When we reduce our desires and fears by the authority of our higher thinking we will increase our happiness to that same degree. Our lives will become free from all that was controlling us before, unbidden emotions of unknown motivations of nature's purposes and not our own. Our wisdom is to know this could now become our new found motivation for happiness and not for just what feels good.

Enlightenment also means the more that is acquired the farther we can see we still have to travel. Then to know this will be a journey that is unending, but the beginning was at wisdom's gates and the barrier to entry. This is about the same time we know we will never have all the answers to all of our questions about ourselves and life. All we can ever hope for is that our questions are getting more informed and our awareness of what we do not know is far and above more important than what we do know now or ever will. We should not let this stop us because this was never going to be easy to have ventured this far already. That is true with all discovery: it's not for the faint of resolve, but the sole influences we have over ourselves to meet those challenges of the unknown with a willingness and confidence we have acquired in life to take any risks we must deem necessary to become better than who we are now.

This is also a subject that no one in their right mind would ever venture to know much less try to write about because it also defines their own ignorance, too. Then to be of the right mindset would mean we have to be like everyone else, but we may have never known someone who was wise. This would mean we should question all of the traditional doctrines. Values and beliefs are a road less traveled for sure, but actually a little pathway of our own thinking to pursue a markedly independent course in thought, thus actions initially guided by the wisdom of the ages and our higher thinking are the worthiest of life's causes. This would be a new way of thinking, that a mind is freed from unbidden desires or fears in order to determine what is meaningful from what was meaningless. This is a mind that owns itself over slavery for even all slaves knew they were not free, but we do not know we are not free to direct ourselves by reason and logic to become the dictator of our own destiny. All wisdom seems to be to have an interest in our awareness before we can ever start to realize the effects of those life decisions.

There are some who have accomplished great knowledge of themselves and life so as to direct themselves to progress to a mental point of competence for their happiness and not the power over others for mutual pleasures. This is a one-way very narrow pathway of life that is hard to find by the evidence of so few to be seen along the way. This will make us doubt ourselves, but once we are on the path of least resistance we are happier. This is the noblest endeavor imaginable; surely others who have spent as much time on this would have advanced this cause more notably. There is nothing left to be done when we have come to realize we are not the doer anyway, it has all been done for us. Now we must know we are in heaven on earth, and our happiness is in the joy of life itself.

It's taken me half my life to get rid of what's meaningless yet there is much to do but the distance is far and I'm growing old. Surely there are those among us who can advance the noblest cause of wisdom, enlightenment and happiness.

Due to the conclusion that pleasure is meaningless because it is not thinking, and happiness is meaningful because it is thinking, most publishing companies know that readers purchase pleasurable reading and that this book may not be profitable. Therefore, it was necessary to self-publish in order to maintain this conclusion. Then without a publishing company's services of a concise marketing plan that consists of: book buyers, review copies, press releases, book stores, libraries, academics, specialty markets, chain buyers, internet and social media website, this book would not be marketed. Then readers would also have to want a more meaningful life other than just the instinctual desire for pleasurable reading. The only way this book could be promoted is if you would pass it on to another after you've read it or tell someone else about it.

Since it is an account of my self-discovery all proceeds received from the sale of this book will be used for promotion and distribution of "Happiness is chosen wisely."

ABOUT THE AUTHOR

All writers will be known, or unknown, by the body of their work and not by the symbols of social status of family, education, or wealth. This is because writers and philosophers are judged by 'the message and not the messenger.'

Anyone's fame or fortune is determined by the masses as evidence of their popularity and social acceptance. We have only to look back on our own history to know of the fallacy of being socially acceptable: Jesus and Socrates were sentenced to death by the public because of their unpopular social philosophies. Buddha deserted his family, wife, and child to become a slacker: antisocial, homeless, and a beggar. Would anyone have read their writing with biographies like those?

To be prejudged by my peers prior to ever having read any of my writing would be a mistake: generating a first impression of a person not on the content or skill of the written word. That is an emotional decision without fact, reason, or logic. That in fact someone who has been in and out of society's established accepted order is quite qualified to know and write about that experience.

After burning out of the engineering and business world at 37 years old, and 60-hour work weeks, Byer bought a sailboat and became a semi self-employed, full-time sail bum for twenty years. A struggling sculptor, he decided to follow his dreams of philosophy and writing for self-discovery that he had been reading and writing about after leaving his professional career. At the age of 64 years, for his own satisfaction, he wrote for 14 years about happiness, since he couldn't find any writers who seemed to know what it was. After his career ended he discovered society's goals of success centered around possession and wealth, that society didn't know how to become happy or what happiness really is other than just trying to perpetuate its own social structural survival, which is driven by our necessities of a desire for pleasure and fear of pain, by passions and not by reason.

www.ingramcontent.com/pod-product-compliance
Lightning Source LLC
LaVergne TN
LVHW041606070426
835507LV00008B/165